Psycho Kitty?

by
Pam Johnson-Bennett
Feline Behavior Consultant

THE CROSSING PRESS
FREEDOM, CALIFORNIA

Dedicated to my husband, Scott, with all of my love

Copyright © 1998 by Pam Johnson-Bennett
Cover design by Tara M. Phillips
Cover photo by Culver Pictures
Interior illustrations by Lewis McClellan
Printed in the U.S.A.

2nd Printing, 1999

For information on bulk purchases or group discounts for this and other Crossing Press titles, please contact our Special Sales Manager at 800-777-1048.

Visit our Web site on the Internet: www.crossingpress.com

Disclaimer: *The alternative healing methods of this book are not meant to take the place of expert veterinary care. When your pet is ill, consult a veterinarian.*

Library of Congress Cataloging-in-Publication Data

Johnson, Pam, 1954-
    Psycho kitty? : understanding your cat's "crazy" behavior / by
Pam Johnson-Bennett.
        p. cm.
    Includes index.
    ISBN 0-89594-909-1 (pbk.)
    1. Cats--Behavior. 2. Cats--Psychology. 3. Animal behavior
therapy. I. Title.
SF446.5.J634   1998
636.8--dc21   98-26916
                                      CIP

Table of Contents

Introduction   5

Chapter One
Missing the Mark—Litter Box Problems   13
  The Domino Effect   15
  Stinky Secrets   23
  Too Little Too Late   30
  Magic Carpets   36

Chapter Two
Tooth and Nail—Aggression   47
  Too Hot Espresso   49
  The Raccoon Incident   59
  Family Counseling   69

Chapter Three
Cats as Interior Decorators—Furniture Scratching   79
  Verticals and Horizontals   84
  Why Spray When You Can Scratch   91
  What's Mine Is Mine   95

Chapter Four
Behaviors They Never Warned You About   100
  Fascinating Faucets   101
  Don't Pet Pickles   111
  Strange Tastes   127
  Do Cats Cry?   134
  A Lesson in Love   146

Final Thoughts   155

Index   157

Acknowledgments

I am continually impressed by the love and loyalty that my clients show to their cats. Through my work, I've had the pleasure of meeting some of the most caring people and the most incredible cats. Thank you all!

I am extremely grateful to all the veterinarians who have so generously offered their guidance throughout my career. I'm very appreciative of the trust you've placed in me when working with your clients.

Thank you, Joe Ed Conn, D.V.M., for being such a good friend.

To Steve Dale, your support has meant everything to me, thank you.

Thanks to Chris Achord and *The Cat Shoppe*, here in Nashville, a "must see" store for anyone visiting Music City.

Thank you, Ginger, you've been an inspiration and a great friend.

A very special thanks to my own cats, you're all the best!

Thank you to everyone at *The Crossing Press* for your hard work and dedication to excellence.

Introduction

You've just adopted a dog—yes, a dog. You call a dog trainer to help the pup overcome some housebreaking problems, or maybe he needs training to stop his aggressive behavior toward strangers. None of your neighbors laugh at you or think you're crazy for calling in a trainer. In fact, they're thrilled at the thought of not having to live next door to an ill-mannered canine. On the flip side, tell your neighbors that you're calling someone to help you work on your cat's litter box or aggression problem and the giggling will reverberate throughout the neighborhood.

Ever since I decided to dedicate my life to helping owners solve their cats' behavioral problems, I've heard every excuse and declaration as to why it can't be done.

"Cats are untrainable!"

"Cats are too independent!"

"Cats do what they please!"

"Cats train their owners!"

Many years ago, when I was a brand new cat owner, I too was under the impression that cats were untrainable. The more familiar I became with my cats, the more I realized that I *could* influence their personalities, strengthen the bond we shared, and correct behavior problems. The way a cat *thinks* began to fascinate me. It began to amaze me how little we know about the beautiful animals so many of us share our lives with.

I came upon this interesting career as a Feline Behavior Consultant, strictly by accident. In trying to solve the periodic behavior problems of my cats, I found myself delving deeper into animal psychology. I didn't want merely to correct what we label as *misbehavior*, I wanted to know *why* my cats did what they did. I started using behavior modification with my cats, then moved on to helping my friends solve their cats' problems. Before I realized it, I soon became a consultant to veterinarians. Each year, more cats are euthanized for behavior problems than for any other reason. That's a very sobering fact.

The most important thing you'll learn from this book is to view the world through the eyes of your cat. That's the secret to solving behavior problems. You can't truly correct a behavior problem until you discover the cause. By trying to see things as your cat does, you'll be able to let go of all those preconceived notions that s/he's misbehaving out of spite.

Let's assume the problem you're experiencing with your cat is in fact behavioral. Here's the order of how things would go if the vet feels a referral to a behaviorist was needed. Note that at the bottom of this chart the Treatment Plan is divided into three sections: *owner, pet,* and *environment*. A behaviorist must look at and evaluate all three in order to provide a complete treatment plan.

In this book, I've used real cases to help illustrate diverse points of view: the frustrated owner, the kitty culprit, skeptical family members, and confused companion pets. Also, I hope this approach will help you feel that you're not the only one going

BEHAVIOR PROBLEM

Veterinarian Appointment
physical exam, observation,
lab work, additional tests

Diagnosis
discussion of options,
referral to behaviorist

BEHAVIOR CONSULTATION

Behavioral Diagnosis/Prognosis

TREATMENT PLAN

Owner
education and
possible behavior
modification

Pet
behavior modification
and use of drug
therapy if needed

Environment
modification
if needed

FOLLOW-UP

through a particular problem with a cat. Very often, when I visit a new client, they're shocked to learn that other owners have had a similar crisis. It helps to know you're not alone.

If you're dealing with a behavior crisis right now, I'm going to make two very important requests. First, if you've been disciplining your cat for the misbehavior, I want you to stop. Punishment doesn't work. I repeat, it doesn't work! In fact, it can have the reverse effect and make a bad situation worse. Now I know you've probably been told to rub your cat's nose in his accidents when he doesn't use the litter box, or to thump her nose with your fingers when she tries to bite. Wrong, wrong, wrong. Physical punishment can elevate aggression because it increases the animal's fear. A cat who is aggressive is already in an agitated state and by physically punishing him you could cause him to become more defensive. Hitting a cat also causes confusion because he won't know if the hand coming close to him each time is going to hit or pet him. He'll soon learn to associate your hands with pain and become afraid of you. Not exactly the effect you were looking for, huh?

The other common punishment inflicted on cats, rubbing their noses in their own excrement, is one of the most horribly destructive things you can do. You won't be teaching your cat that urinating outside of his box is bad, you'll be teaching her that *urinating is bad, period!* It will cause her so much stress that you'll only worsen an already serious problem.

WHAT PUNISHMENT ACCOMPLISHES

- confusion in the cat as to why he's being punished
- fear and avoidance of the owner
- continued undesirable behavior in the absence of the owner
- additional behavior problems as a result of counterproductive discipline

---

Through the reports of my housecalls, you'll see the mistakes some owners make and how, with the correct behavior modification, we get the damaged cat/owner relationship back in sync. Sometimes it takes a while, depending upon how long the problem was allowed to go on before help was sought, but in most cases, the bond between owner and cat can be repaired and strengthened.

If you bought this book because your cat is displaying a behavior problem, then you are both probably living under tension. You look over at your kitty and picture the sweet, wonderful cat he used to be. Nowadays though, he's like a cat possessed. You think to yourself, *why is he doing this?* From the other side of the room, your kitty looks over at you with the same confusion, the same questions. The problem is *communication between the two of you.* You're not speaking the same language. Realistically, no matter how smart your cat may be, chances are slim to zero that she's about to learn your language—I'm afraid it's up to you to learn hers. That's where I come in. The stories assembled in this book will help you see the situation from the cat's point of view, and it's very enlightening. The bonus here is that once you understand the cat's vantage point, you can apply that knowledge to solving future behavior problems with your cat. Hopefully though, you'll use the knowledge to head off problems before they even develop.

One term you'll see repeatedly throughout this book is *play therapy*. Those of you familiar with my previous books know the value I place on playing with your cat. In *Twisted Whiskers: Solving Your Cat's Behavior Problems*, I devoted an entire chapter to discussing in depth, the great impact playtime can have on behavior problems. Basically, play therapy involves using an *interactive* toy (a fishing-type pole, string, little toy dangling on the end). I like interactive toys instead of the little furry mice toys that get thrown on the floor and forgotten, for several reasons. First, the interactive toy allows you to do just that: *interact* with your cat. It's a wonderful way to strengthen the bond, build trust, help a timid cat blossom, or speed up the acceptance process between your cat and a new family member. Interactive play is also extremely valuable in dealing with aggressive cats because it redirects the aggression toward the toy at the end of the string, instead of at you. Also, the fishing pole keeps your hand at a safe distance from the cat's teeth.

If you're familiar with my training methods, you know that I use a *positive* approach to correcting behavior and interactive toys are my secret weapons. Since a cat is a predator, it's very hard for one to resist the sight of a bird flying by or a mouse scurrying across the floor. A cat engaged in an unacceptable behavior can usually be distracted with an interactive toy.

Redirecting the aggressive behavior toward the toy makes a negative situation positive. It may seem as if you're rewarding negative behavior, but you aren't. What you're doing is retraining the cat. For example, say your newly adopted cat is about to pounce on your unsuspecting 12-year old cat who is innocently sleeping on the chair. Perhaps the new cat hasn't yet fully accepted his new home or your resident cat, so he often stalks and pounces on her when she's unaware. You could yell at the new cat, smack him on the nose, or chase him into another room, but all that will do is convince him beyond a shadow of a doubt that he was right to hate your cat. They'll never become friends. But if you redirect the behavior toward the toy, you'll distract him from his stalking. The predator in him would much rather chase the little mouse on the end of the toy than get into a fight with your other cat. Moreover, through this distraction, you also allow the new cat to begin associating positive things—such as getting more play time—with the presence of the other cat.

Interactive toys should be standard cat-owning equipment, as much so as litter boxes and food. One word of caution though: be sure to put the toys away when playtime is over to ensure that your cat doesn't chew the strings. The toys are more special the next time they're brought out for play therapy. You'll learn more about the different uses of play therapy throughout this book.

"My cat isn't normal!" I hear these words from owners all the time. Perhaps you too suspect that your own cat isn't normal. Let's take a minute and try to figure out if your cat really is crazy. Behavior problems fall into two categories: *normal* and *abnormal*. Most owners are convinced that their cats belong in the abnormal category. For the most part, they're wrong. Oh, there are surely cats with abnormal problems, but most of the misbehaviors you'll experience with your cat will be the normal kind. I know you don't believe me right now, but it's true. Let's say your cat has rejected her litter box and is urinating and defecating on the carpet behind the sofa. Is that normal? If you said no, you'd be wrong. It is, in fact, a normal behavior. No, I'm not crazy, just stick with me on this. If the cat feels she can't use the litter box for whatever reason (i.e., a medical problem, dirty litter box, emotional reasons, a territorial problem with another cat in the house, etc.), she'll pick a spot that offers her a feeling of comfort or safety. Now, just because I said that the behavior is normal, doesn't mean that it's acceptable. But, by realizing the behavior is the cat's normal reaction to a crisis, you can begin to solve the problem by finding the cause. Let's take the example of a litter box that's too dirty. Look at it in human terms: you're traveling by car and stop at the service station so you can use the restroom. When you go inside you discover it to be filthy. You opt to get back in the car and try the service station across the street. Well, your cat doesn't have that option. If he goes to his litter box and finds it too filthy to use, he may feel the need, if desperate enough, to find a cleaner area. By recognizing that your cat is trying to solve a problem the only way he knows how, you'll hopefully abandon your old belief that he's deliberately being stupid, spiteful, or defiant. Changing your interpretation of his behavior will enable you to identify the possible causes more accurately.

Another example of normal (but again, unacceptable) behavior in a cat is scratching the furniture. Scratching is a normal and essential part of cat life. Instead of punishing your cat, once you realize the behavior is normal and not deliberately destructive, you can set up a more acceptable scratching surface.

Truly abnormal behaviors do exist (an example might be a cat who exhibits unprovoked extreme aggression, perhaps due to a medical cause such as a chemical imbalance). These conditions require your cat to be under the veterinarian's care, perhaps in conjunction with a behaviorist.

For the most part, the behavior problems you'll encounter will be normal, though that won't necessarily make them seem any less frustrating. But now that we've laid the groundwork, you can approach the problem in a more positive way. Look at your cat's world through his eyes and you'll probably find the solution right in front of you.

I hope you enjoy these stories of some of my housecalls. Perhaps in one of them you'll see a situation similar to one of your own. At least you'll know you're not alone and that your cat isn't really crazy after all.

CHAPTER ONE

Missing the Mark—
Litter-Box Problems

For cat owners, I don't think there's a more misunderstood or more complex problem than when a cat stops using the litter-box. It's also a very heartbreaking situation because many owners, convinced this is a problem based on a willful decision to misbehave, seem intent on disciplining their cats. It's also heartbreaking because sometimes cat owners are so sure that this is a *behavior* problem they may neglect to take their cat to the vet. This can result in a worsening of the behavior because there may be a medical cause. What does this mean for the cat? Punishment for something he can't control, added to the increased pain and discomfort he's suffering from the medical condition. If it is, in fact, a medically related behavior and it goes unchecked, it can result in the cat's death. This should be of particular concern for owners of male cats because they are more prone to urinary problems due to the male urethra being longer and more narrow than the female's. Left unchecked, this can result in a total blockage making the passage of urine impossible.

Litter-box problems run the full range, from a cat refusing to use the new brand of litter you just put in the box, to a cat who ignores her litter-box because she's in the midst of a territorial dispute with another cat.

The order to attack this problem is in three stages:

1. *Make sure the problem isn't medical (for example, lower urinary tract disease, renal failure, diabetes, geriatric conditions).*

2. *Check out the box itself. Is it clean? Did you change brands of litter? Is the box too small or covered? Is it in a high traffic area? Is it located too far away? Is there an adequate number of boxes?*

3. *Look for potential emotional causes: death, divorce, new baby, new pet, house renovation, change in owner's schedule—any crisis or change, however insignificant it may seem at the time.*

Certain behavior problems are hard to tackle on your own and litter-box rejection is one of them. Don't hesitate to consult with your vet. He or she may also need to refer you to a behaviorist.

The Domino Effect

Gretchen, a one-year old, 13-pound Maine Coon, sat perched on the lap of one of her owners. Of the two owners, Eddie and Evelyn Clegg, Gretchen had wisely chosen Eddie—he had the larger of the two laps to rest on. Gretchen's large frame and abundant fur created quite a presence. Yet, despite her size, she appeared nervous and apprehensive as I watched her eyes intensely remain fixed on the five-month old lab mix puppy who was busily chewing on a toy, across the room.

I had been called to the Clegg household because Gretchen had stopped using her litter-box since the arrival of young Domino.

"We thought we were doing a good thing," explained Evelyn, as she sadly watched Domino who was happily chewing away on his toy, totally unaware of the chaos he had created since his arrival one month ago. Probably, from his point of view, life was an exciting adventure to be embraced with gusto. He wanted to be friends with everybody and hadn't yet gotten the hint that Gretchen didn't share his enthusiasm.

Eddie and Evelyn, both in their mid-60s, had moved to Nashville two years ago from California. Their daughter's husband had been transferred here and being a close family, the Cleggs wanted to be nearby. They had waited so long to be grandparents that they didn't want to miss watching their two-year old grandson grow up.

"We never had a cat before," said Eddie, as he gently stroked Gretchen. She closed her eyes in enjoyment for a moment, then quickly turned a watchful eye back on the puppy. "We used to have a dog when Laurie was a child, but things sure are different with a cat," he shook his head and smiled.

Evelyn, who was seated on the couch next to me, leaned closer. "Laurie thought it was time we had another pet. She loves cats, so in she walks one day with this kitten for us. Eddie didn't care for the kitten at first."

Eddie interrupted. "That's not true," he defended himself.

"Edward William Clegg, that first night you said the kitten could stay in the kitchen but had to go back the next morning," she shot back at her husband.

"That's how *you* remember it," he sat up straight and Gretchen released her stare on Domino just long enough to check on her owner. Eddie gave her a reassuring pat and she went back to puppy patrol.

Evelyn straightened some imaginary wrinkles on her skirt and then pointed her finger at her husband. Her smile and a wink of her eye let me know that this exchange was all in good-natured fun. Evelyn continued on with her story, "Gretchen wouldn't leave Eddie alone. She followed him everywhere. It was as if she knew she had to win him over," her face softened considerably, "They've been inseparable ever since."

Though Eddie tried to fight it, a grin broke out across his broad face as he looked down at Gretchen.

"I rest my case," declared Evelyn.

So initially, all was wonderful in the Clegg home when little Gretchen became a member of the family. With their daughter's guidance, Eddie and Evelyn set up a litter-box and scratching post. She instructed them on how to feed the new kitten, and she bought them a vast array of cat toys.

For months, life went along smoothly for everyone. According to Evelyn, Gretchen was blossoming into a beautiful cat with perfect manners.

Things changed with the sudden appearance of Domino.

"It all started because *he* gained too much weight," accused Evelyn sternly as she pointed at her husband.

Eddie rolled his eyes in disgust. I shifted in my seat, expecting this to turn into a sensitive exchange between the two of them. The weight of one's spouse can be a touchy subject and I didn't want to be brought into the middle.

"You got fat, admit it, will you?" Evelyn continued, "The doctor said so." Her voice got just a bit louder for emphasis.

"And you've never gained weight?" He asked with a cutting edge. He added, mocking her, "Eddie, do I look fat in this dress? Eddie, do my hips look big? Eddie..."

Evelyn broke in, "Enough!"

I told you, the weight of one's spouse...scary subject.

Eddie sank back in his seat, waving his wife off with his hand. Gretchen, sensing the tension, decided to find other accommodations. With a quick glance at Domino (who was now asleep in his bed), she jumped from Eddie's lap and made a speedy exit out of the room.

"See what you've done?" Eddie said to Evelyn as he pointed toward the retreating cat.

Evelyn chose to ignore his comment and turned her attention back to me. "Anyway," she went on, despite the obvious look of good-natured disapproval on her husband's face. "Eddie has put on forty pounds since we moved here so his doctor put him on a strict diet. He also recommended that Eddie get some exercise every day, specifically, walking. Well, he did it for a week and then gave up. He said it was too boring. So, Laurie decided to get him a puppy. That way they could go on walks together."

According to Evelyn, Eddie looked forward to his walks with Domino. On the other hand, the arrival of Domino had not been such a success with Gretchen.

Evelyn gave a tour of the house and showed me the spots that Gretchen chose repeatedly as her impromptu litter-boxes. Both spots were in the dining room, under the dining table.

The litter-box was located in the bathroom, wedged between the vanity and the tub.

I spent time individually with Gretchen and with Domino. I found Gretchen to be a sweet, playful cat. Domino was, well, a typical friendly, curious puppy looking for a good time. When the two animals were together though, Domino continually trespassed beyond what was obviously Gretchen's comfort zone. Evelyn explained the pattern: he'd run up to her, looking to play, only to be greeted by hisses and growls. Gretchen would then flee, usually retreating to a bedroom, where she'd hide under the bed until the coast was clear. The more Domino tried to make friends, the more Gretchen rejected him. Evelyn and Eddie were understandably upset.

As we walked through the house, Domino followed closely at our heels, determined not to be left out of the adventure. When we reached the bathroom where Gretchen's litter-box was, Evelyn, Eddie and I stepped inside but Domino paused at the doorway, backed up and sat with his front paws just over the threshold. I noticed the expression on his face had changed dramatically. He appeared to be sulking. I asked the Cleggs about the behavior.

"We trained him to stay out of the room," Eddie answered. "He used to bother Gretchen when she was in her box so now he's not allowed in. He's good about it, too. He just lays in the hallway right outside the door and watches her."

"Does he follow her often in here?" I asked as I looked again at Domino, who was now standing in the hallway, wagging his tail.

Evelyn nodded.

"We're trying to train him. He's beginning to get the hang of it, but I guess not soon enough for Gretchen," Eddie added, referring to the housesoiling.

As we walked back to the living room, Domino stopped, preferring to settle in the middle of the hall, halfway between the bathroom and the living room.

"Has he done that before?" I asked, pointing back at Domino.

"Yeah," Eddie replied. "I think he likes the coolness of the floor."

Just then, Gretchen came out of the bedroom and turned in the direction of the hallway. When she saw Domino she stopped in her tracks. Domino's ears perked up and his tail began to wag. He was hoping for a game. Gretchen did an about-face and trotted into the living room. She settled on the highest perch, the headrest of the recliner. Domino's tail gave two hesitant wags before the puppy sank back down to the floor.

The pieces were coming together.

I explained to Evelyn and Eddie that Gretchen didn't feel safe using her litter-box because of Domino. Initially, he had been barging into the bathroom and startling her while she was in the midst of using her box. Being in the litter-box puts a cat in a very vulnerable position. While the Cleggs had done a good job of training Domino to stay out of the bathroom, his presence nearby still posed a threat.

"Being in the litter-box with Domino eagerly standing at the bathroom doorway would still create a sense of fear," I explained. "In addition," I continued while walking into the hallway to illustrate a point, "there are some subtle behaviors taking place here in the hall that are causing serious problems."

I went on to explain that although Domino looked relaxed and innocent as he lounged in the middle of the hallway, he was blocking Gretchen's safe passage to the litter-box. I felt that Domino chose to camp out there because he knew this was a sure way not to miss the cat, should she go by. The problem was that Gretchen soon became too intimidated to pass. Therefore, her only option was to find a safer place for her eliminations. And it wasn't merely coincidence that her choice was in the dining room. This was the one room with three entrance/exit ways: one to the kitchen, another to the living room, and a third to the hallway. By going under the dining table, Gretchen felt hidden, but the openness of the room provided her with a wide visual field. There'd be enough reaction time should she see Domino. The litter-box in the bathroom was beside the vanity, hidden from the door so Gretchen wouldn't know if Domino was approaching until it was too late.

"In a multi-pet home, you have to be careful you don't hide the litter-box so far into a corner that it makes a cat feel helplessly trapped," I explained to the Cleggs as we stood in the dining room. "Look at the setup from your cat's point of view." I pointed to the different vantage points that the dining room offered.

"Does that mean we have to put the litter-box under the dining room table?" asked a grim-faced Evelyn.

I shook my head, much to everyone's relief.

Treatment Plan

The first thing I did was get out my black light in order to check for any urine spots that may have been overlooked. A black light has a special bulb that causes urine stains to fluoresce. Black lights are available from most pet supply stores, and some even rent them. The lights are also available through mail order.

I marked the spots on the carpet that the Cleggs had missed by placing pieces of tape over each stain. This way we could locate them when I turned the black light off. I then used a liquid enzyme product on the areas to completely neutralize the odor and eliminate the stain. It's essential that you use a product that specifically states that it neutralizes the odor. Regular household or carpet cleaners get out the stain but they may only mask the odor. Just because it smells clean to you doesn't mean your cat can't detect the odor. Remember a cat's nose is much more sensitive than a human's.

After we cleaned the carpet under the dining table and absorbed as much moisture as possible with towels, I directed a small fan over the spot to accelerate the drying time. Once the carpet was dry, I stacked boxes under the table to prevent Gretchen from going back there. It would look funny for a while, I told the Cleggs, but it was only temporary.

Next on the list was to add a second litter-box in a location that would provide Gretchen with the same level of comfort she felt in the dining room. The Cleggs had a spare bedroom that had been converted into an extra storage area. I suggested we put a litter-box in there. The box was to be placed away from the wall and not wedged in a corner. I wanted Gretchen to feel she had several escape options. I also instructed the Cleggs to install a baby gate across the doorway. This way, Gretchen could easily go in and out of the room. With the help of obedience training, the gate would keep Domino out of Gretchen's area. For convenience, using a gate that swings open would make it easy for Evelyn and Eddie to go in and out of the room. As Domino became trained to stay out of the room, the gate could eventually come down. For now though, it would provide a little comfort for Gretchen.

By having a litter-box in two locations on opposite ends of the house, Gretchen would have another option should Domino block her path to one of them.

To help acquaint Gretchen with her new area, we placed a little of the soiled litter from her initial box into the new box. Then, after feeding Gretchen, Eddie would gently carry her into the spare bedroom. There, he would sit at the desk and read while Gretchen sniffed around, becoming familiar with the new surroundings. Since Gretchen was closely bonded with Eddie, having him in the room might make her feel more at ease.

Creating a safe, comfortable sanctuary for Gretchen in that extra bedroom could provide the relief she would need when the puppy wouldn't leave her alone. To accomplish this, we brought in two cat trees. One was placed in the bedroom by the window (which soon became known as "Gretchen's room") and the other was set up in the living room. The reason I wanted one there was so Gretchen could stay in the room with her owners even if she didn't want to be bothered by Domino.

Treatment Plan (continued)

I instructed the Cleggs on how to engage in play sessions with Gretchen to redirect her focus if she started to get nervous around Domino. They were also to continue training the puppy to respond to voice commands so they could control him before he stepped over the line with the cat. Using a dog trainer would help make Domino a well-behaved pet and would help cut down on future problems. I gave the Cleggs the names of two trainers I regularly work with.

Follow Up

Providing an additional litter-box for Gretchen made all the difference. She had no problem hopping over the gate and has used both litter-boxes faithfully. The boxes in the dining room were removed after one week.

The cat trees were a blessing for Gretchen while she was still unsure about Domino's intentions. She'd sit at the top of the tree in the living room and observe him. Eventually, she'd sneak down to get a closer look, but knowing she could quickly be out of his reach made her feel secure and accelerated her acceptance of him.

By engaging in regular play-therapy sessions with Gretchen, and using the services of a trainer for Domino, harmony in the Clegg house has been restored.

Six months later, the baby gate was removed.

Stinky Secrets

Litter-box rejection is the most common problem for which I'm consulted. In almost every case, the owner believes the cat is misbehaving out of spite. I try to impress upon clients that it causes the cat a great deal of stress when he feels he can't use his litter-box. Owners are always surprised by this fact. Cats inherently eliminate away from the nest, so for him to urinate on the living room carpet means he feels he has *no other choice*—he's desperate!

Margaret Christensen was one of those owners who was convinced that Stinky, her nine-month old Persian was suddenly becoming spiteful.

"I spoke with the breeder," Margaret said during our initial phone conversation. "She said that Stinky had been easy to litter train. I don't know why he's doing this."

During our conversation I asked Margaret if she'd taken Stinky to the vet to have his urine checked. Yes, she said, she'd done all of that and the vet said there was nothing wrong.

Margaret began to first notice a problem when Deborah, one of her three teenage daughters, mentioned that she saw Stinky urinating in the laundry basket. Filled with dirty clothes, the basket was sitting next to the washer. Deborah's discovery made Margaret recall that she routinely thought she smelled an odor similar to cat urine whenever she was in the laundry room. At the time, she had dismissed it as being a bad combination of odors from the piles of soiled laundry. After Deborah's discovery, Margaret whisked Stinky off to the vet for an exam.

Stinky's physical exam revealed him to be in perfect health, so I was the next one Margaret called, on the recommendation of her vet.

"I didn't realize the problem had gotten so bad," she told me over the phone, "until I was opening the windows in the sunroom. I smelled something nasty. I looked around and found piles of cat poop in the corner behind the potted plants."

Margaret had thought she'd solved Stinky's litter-box problem by replacing the laundry basket with a hamper. No one in the family had reported any accidents so she figured all was normal again. This recent discovery of cat poop changed everything.

When I arrived at the Christensen house, I was greeted by the entire family. Margaret and her husband, Phil, had asked that the three daughters be a part of the session since they interacted the most with Stinky.

As we walked through the foyer toward the family room, we passed the kitchen, where I noticed a woman busily working away. A wonderful aroma of freshly baked chocolate chip cookies came from that direction. My stomach groaned in approval. Margaret caught me enjoying the aroma. "Maria comes three days a week to do the cleaning and she always bakes for us," she said.

I nodded, noticing that the little bit of the house I had seen so far was certainly spotless, and there was a slight scent of lemon furniture polish in the air.

At first my discussion with the Christensen family yielded nothing remarkable. No, there had been no changes to the house… all schedules were basically consistent…no recent traumas or stressful situations had come up. Basically, Stinky was a happy cat (or so they thought), living in a home with five very loving family members.

"When was the last time Stinky didn't use the litter-box?" I asked.

"Other than the laundry basket, which I took away, it was three days ago when I found the cat poop in the sunroom," Margaret said, adding that she had scolded the cat.

"So, it's been very sporadic?" I asked, directing the question toward the entire family.

Phil shrugged. "It must be. We haven't found evidence of anything."

"Tell me about his litter-box habits," I asked. "How often does he go, and do you notice anything particular about his behavior when he actually does use the box?"

I watched as the various members looked from one to the other. Deborah volunteered an answer. "I don't really ever see him in his box very much. He's pretty modest, I guess." With that, the other family members nodded in agreement.

"Who routinely cleans the box?"

"We all scoop it out," Margaret replied, "I insisted that everyone be responsible for scooping each time they pass by."

As I continued my questioning it seemed that no one could remember the last time they'd scooped anything out of the litter-box. With so many people doing it, they each assumed someone else had already gotten to it and that's why the box was always clean. But *somebody* had to have scooped *something*, yet no one could remember doing so. This wasn't a good sign.

The best place to start with this mystery was with the box itself. In my usual routine, touring the house and viewing the litter-box is essential.

My antenna immediately went up as we entered the guest bathroom, where the litter-box was kept.

"This is Stinky's room. No one else uses it," Margaret proudly assured me as she turned on the light. What I saw was a major infraction of Rule #1 in Cat Etiquette. Stinky's litter-box, though a good size and very clean, was only inches from his food and water bowls. For life and death reasons, a cat in the wild would never eliminate his waste within his nest area (where cats eat, sleep, play, and raise their young) because it then becomes a huge welcome sign for predators. Even very domesticated indoor cats share that survival instinct. So Stinky became faced with a serious dilemma. He could either eat in the bathroom or he could use his litter-box. Logically, since the food source was only in that one location, it narrowed down his choices. He had to seek out a more appropriate place to eliminate, far away from his food and "nest."

Very often, owners will create an exclusive little area containing the cat's food and litter-box. I had one client who felt this would be a good way to litter train his cat because she'd be visually reminded of her box the second she turned around from the food bowl. The client was shocked to learn that it had the opposite effect.

After explaining to the Christensens the theory behind keeping distance between litter and food, I spent time with Stinky to see if there was anything else going on. He appeared to be somewhat stressed and the best way I can describe it is that he seemed like a cat with a burden on his shoulders. And, he surely did have quite a burden since he never knew where it was acceptable to eliminate.

All of this was beginning to make sense to the Christensen family. They were getting a better understanding of how their cat's mind worked. Everyone was excited about making the necessary changes to help Stinky. One thing still bothered me though. The number of times the owners had discovered an inappropriately placed elimination and the number of times he should've eliminated (based on two meals a day), wasn't adding up. I grilled the owners again as to who had actually cleaned what out of the litter-box over the last several days, and still no one recalled anything specific.

"Stinky has to be going somewhere," I said, with different concerns running through my head. I feared that if we really searched every corner in the house we'd find lots of hidden stains and messes. Margaret's jaw dropped when I voiced my suspicions.

"Well, let's look right away," she demanded as she looked worriedly from one family member to another. "Everyone take a different room."

We all spread out, reminiscent of a bizarre scavenger hunt. Stinky just watched from his perch on the back of the sofa. "Can I at least have a hint?" I quietly whispered as I walked by, stroking his back in passing. He wasn't giving up any secrets.

Half an hour later we were all back, assembled in the living room. None of us having had any success in discovering any of Stinky's secret places. I pulled my keys out of my purse. "I'm going to get the black light out of my car," I said while heading toward the door. "The black light will cause any urine stains to fluoresce, making them much easier to see."

On my way to the front door, I passed the kitchen and absent-mindedly glanced in at Maria, who was busily working away. She quickly looked up at me and then averted her eyes. Was it just my imagination or did she try to avoid making eye contact with me? Don't be silly, Pam, I thought to myself and proceeded toward the front door. Then it hit me. Back into the kitchen I went.

Maria saw me and busied herself all the more. I walked up to her and smiled. She wasn't buying it and refused to return my smile.

"Maria," I began, "Can I ask you a couple of questions about Stinky?"

Maria nodded, yet continued with her work which looked to be just arranging and rearranging objects on the counter. Why was she nervous?

"When you've been doing the cleaning, have you ever come across any of Stinky's messes?" I asked.

She answered quickly, "No."

"Are you sure?" I prodded.

Maria was silent for a moment, then looked toward the kitchen entrance before leaning closer to me. "I don't want to get Stinky in trouble," she whispered. "I love him and I'm afraid they'll put him to sleep."

"So you *have* cleaned up after him?"

"Yes, many times," she answered while looking down. "He never uses his box. He always goes in the sunroom. I know all of his favorite spots so I clean them as soon as I get here."

I put my hand on Maria's shoulder and told her not to worry. Stinky wasn't going to be put to sleep and now I had the information I needed to help him. Maria's face suddenly lit up.

I walked back to the Christensen family in the living room, ready to map out a treatment plan. I now had all the pieces of the puzzle. It was confirmed that Stinky wasn't ever using his box.

Treatment Plan

The first order of business was to locate all of Stinky's favorite impromptu "litter-box" areas and thoroughly clean and neutralize the stains. Using the black light, we were able to pinpoint areas that Maria had missed. We used an enzyme liquid specifically designed to neutralize the odor so it wouldn't encourage Stinky to return to those spots.

The sunroom had French doors at the entrance so I felt they should remain closed for a week. I wanted to break the behavior pattern Stinky had set up. For now, the sunroom would be off limits. After a week, it could be opened up again, but with small dishes of dry food sitting on top of the neutralized areas, thus transforming them from a litter-box area to a nest area. The dishes would remain in place for several weeks. I instructed Margaret to remove them gradually one at a time, once Stinky was successfully using his box again.

The food and water bowls were removed from the bathroom and placed in the kitchen. Since Stinky always comes running whenever he hears food hitting the bowl, I instructed Margaret to make a big production out of dinner time. She was to call his name, praise him, and make sure he got accustomed to the new dining location.

After dinner, Margaret was to guide Stinky toward the litter-box (he loved to follow her anyway, so this was easy). Instead of placing him directly in the box, I wanted Margaret to take her finger and scratch around in the litter so Stinky could hear it. I didn't want this to be a big deal and she wasn't to hang around in the bathroom too long. Stinky was to have privacy. He'd soon realize that the smell and sight of food was no longer inappropriately close to his box.

By using interactive toys, the family was to divert Stinky's attention away from the sunroom whenever he started sniffing around. If they even slightly suspected that he was about to relieve himself somewhere other than his box, they were to distract him with a toy. This, I explained, would change his negative feelings into positive feelings. He would become focused on the toy and that would bring about the confidence associated with being a predator. Then, when the mini-game was over, someone could go make a scratching sound in the litter-box. All of this would be low-key. There would be no whisking him off and plunking him in the box, insisting that he stay there and do his business. That method never works and just creates a more stressed cat.

I finally instructed the Christensens to not use any form of punishment should someone come across an accident or actually catch Stinky in the act. Punishment would only make the cat feel that the very act of elimination is bad. He wouldn't understand that he was being punished for his choice of location. Every time he had the urge, he'd become nervous knowing that he might get into trouble. This would result in two things: first, a cat who resorts to finding more obscure locations, and second, a cat who becomes afraid of his owner.

The Christensens felt confident that they could handle the situation, and Maria was visibly relieved that Stinky's life was spared.

Follow Up

By appealing to the cat's instinctual need to eliminate away from the nest, we were able to quickly retrain Stinky. After just a couple of misplaced attempts, he began using his box again. When the sunroom was reopened, Stinky checked out his former locations, smelled the dry food in the dishes that were strategically placed, and never had another accident.

One month after my visit, the last of the food was removed from the sunroom floor.

During my follow-up phone call six months later, I was happy to hear that Stinky was using his litter-box and spent much of his days trying to steal the food that Maria painstakingly spent preparing for the family.

Too Little Too Late

I made a housecall to Barbara Cunningham's home to address a litter-box problem concerning her three cats. All three cats had decided to stop using the box and elected to go on the floor beside it instead.

I went through all the usual questions with Barbara on the phone. She'd already had all three cats checked by the vet, she had more than one litter-box, and she routinely cleaned them all. She hadn't had any change in her life recently. So we set up an appointment.

Now there have been times in my career in which clients have tried to convince me that they should come to my office rather than have me come to their homes. They say it would increase the number of clients I could see. Even some behaviorists believe housecalls are unnecessary; they believe you can learn all you need to know from an office visit. To them, I say, "No way." Here's a case that proved that I was correct in my decision to make housecalls. If ever, on a cold or rainy night when I'm driving to a housecall and wishing I had office hours instead, I will remember Barbara Cunningham's three cats.

When I entered the house, I was greeted by Barbara, a very attractive, well-dressed woman who looked to be in her mid-40s. Behind her stood her husband and two teenage sons. They were all looking forward to a visit with the cat shrink to uncover their cats' strange emotional disorder.

The three Himalayan cats, all littermates, purchased from a breeder, were nowhere to be seen. "They spend much of their time sleeping," offered Barbara as she noticed me looking around.

Barbara insisted on bringing me immediately to the litter-boxes to view the "scene of the crime," as she put it. Now, there are times when cats stop using their litter-box for emotional reasons, and it takes a lot of work on my part to figure out what went wrong. Then there are the cases like this one, where all it took was looking at the litter-box conditions. The reason for the behavior was immediately apparent and the solution was simple. I hadn't even taken my coat off or put my briefcase down, when I had the answer. I stood before two litter-boxes, three feet apart in a combination laundry room /mudroom. The boxes themselves were uncovered (thank goodness for that, at least), but they were very tiny. Now with boxes that small, one would think that the cats must be on the small side but Himalayans aren't known for being petite.

Even when I feel I know what the problem is right off the bat, I keep it to myself and keep an open mind until I've gone through the whole procedure of interviewing the owners and spending time with the cats. There's always a chance that I'll be given new information that will alter my theory. This was not the case with the Cunninghams. Upon interviewing the family, I learned that all three cats got along beautifully. At nine months old, they all played, slept, and ate together. Their spay surgery three months prior had gone smoothly, without so much as a hiss from anybody upon returning home from the hospital.

It was clear to me that making a housecall was necessary because the information Barbara provided me with on the phone didn't match what I was seeing. I had asked her on the phone about the size and location of the boxes and she had said they were big and far apart in different rooms. What I learned when I got there was that she viewed the *laundry* part of the room as a separate area from the *mud* section. To me, it was still one room. And, as for litter-box size, one person's impression of *big* is different from another's.

When it came time to meet Ling Ling, Ming, and Yoki, I was not surprised to see three very massive mountains of fur. When I entered the sunny bedroom where they spent the bulk of their time, I was greeted with a mildly curious look by each, before they decided I wasn't interesting enough for any further investigation. All three cats laid their heads back down and continued their naps.

Needing to be sure that they were just sedentary and not depressed, I got out my toys and managed to entice them into play. Of course I had to wait until all three had sufficiently yawned, stretched, and consulted with each other. Once the formalities were out of the way, they indulged me and we enjoyed a low-key play-therapy session.

After interviewing the family and my play-therapy session with the cats, my original theory as to the cause of the inappropriate elimination held. Basically, it came down to common sense (or lack of it). Here were the facts: three big cats with lots of *output* and two tiny litter-boxes with too much *input*. Added to that problem, there was an insufficient amount of litter in each box. The solution involved a few basic steps, and once again, common sense. How could Barbara's family not register how dirty and inadequate the litter-boxes were? The house itself appeared clean and very nicely furnished. So what happened when it came to the litter-box? My theory was "out of sight, out of mind." Litter-box maintenance isn't one of our favorite things to do, so, we look for all kinds of ways to reduce our exposure to it. It only takes looking through a cat magazine at the dozens of ads for all the latest self-cleaning boxes (I'm not kidding), new improved litters, liners, disposable boxes, toilet-training products (a very bad idea, trust me), litter additives, even long-handled scoops to use so you don't have to get close to the soiled litter. You can find litter-boxes disguised as planters, fancy screens for your kitty's privacy, oh, the list goes on. It's big business. Why? Because we *hate* to clean the litter-box. That's why Barbara Cunningham put two small boxes in the back part of the house that no one in the family really uses. Barbara informed me that no one comes in through the mudroom door. She's the only one who goes back there to do laundry three times a week.

The scooping routine they had set up when the cats were kittens was adequate when it came to scooping, but what the Cunninghams didn't take into consideration was the increased amount of waste that the cats would produce as they got bigger. Barbara didn't adjust the size of the boxes or the cleaning schedule as her cats grew. This brought up another point that we would still have to address—her cats were too heavy.

"I read on the bag of litter that you had to scoop only once a day," Barbara stated as I began to tell her my assessment.

"You have to adjust everything you do based on your individual situation," I explained. With three large cats and two small boxes, they're getting filled up more often. That's why the cats are going outside of the box. They're eliminating as close as possible to where they're supposed to."

I explained to Barbara and her family that they were fortunate that the three cats didn't appear too stressed yet, although I know they weren't pleased with the situation. They had found a solution to the problem by using the floor around the box. It was the best option they had.

Treatment Plan

The two small boxes were fine when Barbara's cats were kittens but now that they were fully grown, she needed to make changes. I recommended getting two larger boxes. They certainly had the space in the laundry/mudroom to do that. I would've preferred to have another box on the second floor of the house because I believed there should be a box on each floor but Barbara's husband wouldn't budge on that point. So, we'd have to make due with the one location.

Treatment Plan (continued)

Next came the amount of litter. Apparently, Barbara, once again was following the directions on the bag, but not paying attention to the fact that she had three cats who produced a large volume of urine and spent a great deal of effort to push the small amount of litter into the corner in an attempt to cover it. Barbara needed to sufficiently cover the bottom of the pan with a good layer of litter. A general rule of thumb is a two-inch layer as a good starting point. You then make adjustments based on your cat's litter habits.

Next, we discussed the most crucial part of litter-box mainte-nance—cleaning. The boxes had to be scooped several times a day. To make it more manageable, I felt the task shouldn't just fall to Barbara, but that everyone should be responsible for routine scooping.

Since no one but Barbara ever really ventured back to the laundry area, I suggested that there be set times for litter-box checking to help them develop a routine. For instance, first thing in the morning, after lunch, or when the kids come home from school, and last thing at night. Basically, they just needed to work out a system to remind themselves to check the litter-boxes. Whether they posted a note on the refrigerator, or assigned times to each family member didn't mat-ter as long as it got done.

Finally, we discussed nutrition. I learned that the cats were being fed home-cooked meals based on the breeder's suggestion. I recom-mended that she talk to her vet about changing her cats over to a pre-mium veterinary diet. A home-cooked diet is a dangerous route to go if you don't know what you're doing.

Specific instructions on play therapy for all three cats were also part of the treatment plan. I wanted each cat to have at least a twice-daily session, consisting of a minimum of 15 minutes each. These cats were too young to be this obese.

Follow Up

That was all it took. Barbara went out that evening to purchase new boxes and initiated a family scooping schedule. There have been no accidents since.

Ling Ling, Ming, and Yoki are now off the home-cooked meals and on a diet of top-quality cat food. The changeover in diet and the play therapy have helped them to slim down. Without all that extra weight, the cats have become more active and interact with the family more.

The lesson here is that sometimes we all need a reminder about common sense. I can think of lots of other things I'd rather do than scoop the litter-box, but it needs to be done and my cats count on me.

We also need to remember to make adjustments as our cats grow and change. Matching your cat's litter-box to his size, age, and physical health is important. For example, a very tall cat will probably feel too cramped in a covered litter-box. A tiny kitten may have trouble climbing over the side of a jumbo box, so you may have to start with a low-sided box and change it as he grows. A geriatric cat with arthritis may no longer be able to hop up into a high-sided box and may need a box with lower sides.

Magic Carpets

There are cats who go through life without any problems. They are the cats who, despite mistakes we as owners make, never urinate outside of the litter-box, scratch the furniture, hiss at the baby, or bite the hand that feeds them.

Then there are the cats who don't handle life's bumpy roads very well. Survival for them becomes a constant challenge to overcome the threat of the *unexpected*. The sound of the hair dryer or the sudden appearance of a pillow that falls off the bed can be enough to convince certain cats that every room in the house contains psychological land mines. *Cats hate change, cats hate change, cats hate change!* I repeat this to owners so often during the day that I'm sure I probably mumble it in my sleep as well.

Because we never know which bump in the road might be the one that our cats can't get over, we do the best we can to gradually expose them to necessary changes. Most of the time it works, but sometimes that little bump turns out to be a stone wall.

I had to give a public education seminar last year to benefit a local humane organization. When I walked in, I noticed that the room was quite crowded and was delighted to see how many people were interested in learning more about feline behavior. I never know what to expect when I do these seminars because the topic still causes much giggling and snickering. So when I saw that every seat was filled, I felt myself getting charged up.

Although I cover as many basics as I can during a two-hour lecture, I always start out by asking people what types of problems they're having. By asking for a show of hands, I inquire as to how many are experiencing problems with: litter-box, aggression toward people, aggression toward companion pets, scratching furniture, stress/anxiety, jealousy, depression, finicky eating, and general training problems.

Now, normally, the majority of hands will go up in response to this variety of problems. By asking for a show of hands, I know how deeply I'll need to go into a topic, or if I can skim over it. This night every hand went up when I mentioned the litter-box. I scanned the room very carefully to make sure I wasn't missing anyone, but as I looked around, everyone was raising a hand in the air. Some hands were held up just inches, perhaps indicating the embarrassment the owners were feeling. Many people were waving their arms over their head and nodding, afraid I wouldn't notice them.

Realizing that we had no time to waste, I put aside my notes on furniture scratching, jealousy, and other behavior problems, and began an in-depth discussion on Feline Inappropriate Elimination (i.e., *Peeing in the wrong places*).

As is usually the case, as I talked with the audience I discovered many of the owners were having problems due to some basic errors, such as: only one box for several cats, unclean boxes, different brands of litter, food too close to the litter, etc. I had easy answers for those owners' questions.

In addition, there were two people at the seminar in search of answers to their litter-box problems who both had something in common: their cats were reacting to the way something felt to their paws. That something was *carpet*. Here are their stories:

Cole Anderson, at 36, was finally at a point in his life when he had enough extra money to make some home improvements. Since his divorce five years ago, Cole had been living with just the basics as he tried to climb out of debt. Now, with a great job and having made better financial decisions, he wanted to freshen up his home and get rid of some of the reminders of what he considered to be his ex-wife's bad taste.

Having grown up around cats, Cole decided the first improvement he needed to make in his home was to once again share his life with a furry friend. His ex-wife had been allergic to cats, so during their six-year marriage, he had accepted the fact that the closest he'd get to having a cat would be to befriend the neighborhood tom who routinely raided his trash cans.

Now, with itchy-eyed Linda gone and the tom having moved on to more interestingly filled trash cans, Cole was in search of a cat. He had no idea what kind of cat he wanted or where to look. The local humane society seemed like the obvious choice, so he planned to visit there right after breakfast one morning.

As he read the morning paper, he took a quick look through the classified section to see if any cats were being given away. Suddenly there she was. Fate, destiny, whatever you want to call it, Cole knew he had found his cat even before seeing her.

> Free to a good home.
> Fifteen-month old
> female Manx cat.
> All shots up to date.
> Playful and affection-
> ate. Must give away.
> Wife allergic.

It was the last two words that caught Cole's eye. *Wife allergic*. He grabbed the phone and dialed the number. He had no idea what a Manx cat was but he didn't care. After all, he thought to himself, as long as she had fur, two ears, whiskers, and a tail, that had to qualify her as a cat.

"Where's her tail?" Cole asked the owners as he stood in the foyer of their home. He'd driven right over as soon as the husband told him the cat was still available.

"She's a Manx," the man answered. "She's not *supposed* to have a tail."

Cole thought, never take anything for granted. Nevertheless, he felt a strong connection to the cat and brought her home.

Winsome took a little while to adjust to her new home. She remained slightly timid for the first two weeks but with time, patience, and a box of cat treats, she warmed up to Cole.

Feeling a bit rusty as a pet owner, Cole brushed up on his knowledge by reading books and seeking advice from friends.

Having planned to begin refurbishing the house before Winsome came into his life, Cole knew he now had to work gradually. He learned that too much change could be scary for a cat and he'd worked hard to develop a close relationship with her. He wasn't about to spoil that.

The home improvement project began with Winsome's needs in mind. Cole painted one room at a time and kept Winsome at the other end of the house while he was doing so. He purchased new furniture for the dining room and living room, a few pieces at a time, and allowed Winsome to play and rub all over each new arrival. Included in his decorating plan was a tall cat tree that would sit in the front window.

All was going well. So far Cole had taken great pains to ease his cat through everything. He was now coming around to the home stretch. The only thing left to do was install wall-to-wall carpeting in the bedroom. Cole decided to spoil himself and go for the expensive plush pile. He imagined it would feel wonderful for his bare feet to sink into the soft carpet every morning when he got out of bed.

What Cole hadn't imagined was that from the moment the carpet was installed, Winsome would begin using it instead of her litter-box.

"I tried to do everything so gradually for her," Cole said, looking around the room for support. "She was fine with the new furniture. She was fine with the painting. She was even fine when that obnoxious decorator came over to measure my windows for drapes. So, *why* does she hate the carpet?"

Obviously, my initial impression was that the change from one owner to another, and the various home improvements had finally taken their toll.

I asked Cole if the cat had been to the vet and what, if any, behavior modification methods did he try. He answered that yes, he had taken Winsome to the vet and the cat was healthy. He also mentioned that he'd read my books and had used an enzyme product to neutralize the odor. He then put food bowls over the spots. He had even followed my play-therapy suggestions.

"Did you cover the carpet at all?"

"I laid plastic sheeting down because she was ruining my brand new carpet," he answered.

"Did she use the litter-box when the carpet was covered?" I asked, walking from the front of the room toward the audience so I could hear his response better.

"She used it every time. Then, as soon as I uncovered the carpet, she went back to her old tricks."

I had a hunch. "Is she declawed?" I asked.

"Yeah," he answered. "I didn't have it done though. The owners before did it."

"Are you using the same kind of litter that the previous owners used?" I asked.

Cole knew where I was leading and was ready. "I use the exact same brand," he replied emphatically.

"Clay litter or scoopable sand?"

"Clay. The other owners used that sand stuff. I like the clay. It's from the same manufacturer though," he replied.

I walked closer to Cole Anderson. He began to look at me suspiciously. I don't have a very imposing presence but he was looking at me as if I might reprimand him. To put him at ease I smiled but then quickly managed to make him uncomfortable again with my next question. "Can you describe Winsome's routine when she's in the litter-box?"

"Her *routine*?" He looked at me with a blank expression. "She pees and she poops. What else is there?"

I pressed on. "Does she spend a lot of time digging before she actually eliminates? Does she cover afterward or does she just hop in, take care of business, and bolt out of there?"

I could see by Cole's expression that I had struck a chord. "She jumps in and perches on the very edge, then jumps right out. Any attempt at covering is done on the floor outside of the box. She never actually covers with the litter."

Treatment Plan

After interpreting the series of events as told by Cole, I had a theory as to what the problem was. Winsome, a declawed cat, was used to the soft feel of the scoopable sand litter. When she went to live with Cole and had to use the rougher clay litter she tried to limit her contact with it. Some common signs that a cat may be uncomfortable with the litter substrate include: perching on the edge of the box, not covering, and then zooming out of there. The cat may also attempt to cover by scratching at the walls or floor around the box. Now, not every cat who doesn't cover is unhappy with the litter, but in Winsome's case the pieces of the puzzle all seemed to fit together.

When Cole installed the soft plush carpet in the bedroom it probably reminded Winsome of the way the sand litter felt. The carpet met all of Winsome's requirements. It was soft, absorbent, and it didn't bother her sensitive paws. Sometimes the paws of declawed cats remain tender long after the surgery and in some cases, for the rest of the cat's life.

My recommendation to Cole was a switch to the scoopable sand litter. "Keep the carpet covered for a while so Winsome has time to make the new connection with the way her paws now feel in the litter-box."

The other interesting carpet-related problem had to do with a woman who was completely at her wit's end with the seven-year old stray she'd adopted two months earlier. Peggy Bosh had tried everything, she said, to train her cat to use a litter-box. "He just won't use it," she said with a sigh. "My vet said there's nothing wrong with him. He just doesn't know what the box is for."

"What training methods have you tried?" I asked.

"Everything!" she answered.

I smiled. "Can you be a bit more specific?"

Peggy had found this smelly, filthy, gray stray cat inside of her car. Just before she was about to go to bed one night she remembered that she'd forgotten to close the car window and it looked like rain. She put her slippers on, threw a robe over herself, and darted out to the driveway. As she opened the door she saw a pair of eyes staring at her from the front seat. At first she was startled but then she saw it was just a skinny little gray cat. The cat hissed at her and then bolted out of the car through the open door.

As Peggy closed the window she thought to herself that she'd have to spray some kind of air freshener in the car tomorrow because it smelled like cat urine.

Padding back toward the house in her fuzzy slippers she was surprised to find the cat sitting on the back porch watching her. She thought for sure he'd run as she got closer, but he held his position. Peggy walked by him and into the house. She was sure he'd be gone in a few minutes.

Just before she was about to go to sleep she took a quick glance outside to see if the cat had gone. There he was, still sitting on the back porch, looking in at her. Peggy turned out the light and went to bed.

It was after the third large boom of thunder that Peggy got out of bed and went back to the kitchen to look out the back door. When she flicked on the light she saw that the driving rain caused the driveway to look more like a river. When she looked onto the back porch she saw the same gray cat staring at her, only this time he was soaking wet.

Despite her better judgment that this action would probably result in having fleas in her carpet, Peggy opened the door and watched the wet cat trot inside.

In her robe and slippers, she searched the basement for the bag of cat litter that she kept for winter emergencies in case her car got stuck in the ice. Having found that, she rummaged some more until she found an old dishpan to use as a litter-box.

Filling the pan with litter, she placed it in the kitchen. She also put down a bowl of water and searched through the refrigerator for some leftover chicken for her guest.

The last thing Peggy did before retiring to bed was to put an old blanket down on the floor for the cat and then close the door that separated the kitchen from the rest of the house. Off to bed she went, not certain, but fairly sure she had just adopted a cat.

After a trip to the vet that included a bath, the gray cat that Peggy adopted turned out to be white.

"The night I found the cat I knew that if I kept him it would be a struggle to teach him house manners and it was," Peggy said. "I've managed to get him to stop stealing my dinner and he's becoming very affectionate, but he just doesn't get the idea of the litter-box. I had him neutered and at the time the vet suggested that I keep him confined in the bathroom with his box. The vet said he'd soon get the hang of what the box was for. He'd hold it until I thought he would burst, and then he'd finally go in the box. To give him the hint, I've even put his poop in the box whenever I find it on the carpet. I've covered the carpet with some plastic shower curtains but he just rips through them to get to the carpet. It's the carpet that he wants to pee on. He doesn't bother with the floor or the throw rugs. He wants my carpet." Peggy stretched up and pointed to Cole Anderson, who was sitting two rows behind her. "Like that gentleman there, I've put food out in several places along the carpet but he just urinates right next to them."

I asked Peggy if she was sure that what Oscar was doing was urinating and not spraying. When a cat sprays he backs up to a vertical object, usually with a twitching tail. With random urination, the cat squats. Both male and female cats normally squat for urination. Male cats don't lift their leg the way male dogs do.

Peggy responded that Oscar was definitely not spraying. He was squatting. His accidents included elimination of solid waste as well. He just didn't want anything to do with the litter-box.

Oscar didn't have accidents in any other part of the house and wasn't the least bit interested in any of the other rugs or the floor. He made the decision that the carpet in Peggy's home office and den was perfect for his needs. He refused to compromise.

Peggy was looking at me with an expression that said she expected a solution in two minutes to a two-month old problem. I'd give it a shot. All eyes were on me.

"With a stray cat, especially one who is as old as Oscar, we obviously have no history. Who knows what he's used for litter throughout his life. Normally, I find that when you bring a stray indoors, they aren't the least bit fussy about what substrate they use. It can be anything from your planters to your pillows. Oscar, it seems, has made his own determination and we can either battle with him or we can let him have his way. I vote for the latter."

Everyone stared at me. Had I lost my mind? Was I suggesting that Peggy allow Oscar to ruin her carpet?

"What are you saying?" she asked with wide eyes.

"Do you have any carpet scraps left over?" I asked.

"Yeah, in the basement," she replied.

"Let's try an experiment," I said, and began to lay out the plan.

Treatment Plan

I suggested that Peggy confine Oscar in the bathroom again for about five days. I wanted her to cut a piece of the scrap and put it in the litter-box. Just the carpet, no litter. Each day she was to sprinkle a little litter over the carpet scrap (replacing the scrap as it got soiled). I advised her not to add too much litter but just sprinkle a small amount as Oscar made the adjustment.

"When he starts to use the box consistently you can let him out, but keep the carpet in your office and den covered with the plastic for another week or so," I instructed.

My plan was that as Oscar began to use the box, Peggy could gradually make the pieces of scrap carpet smaller and smaller. Eventually there'd be more litter and less carpet. This, I felt, would be a gradual and painless transition for Oscar.

I qualified my recommendations to both Cole and Peggy by adding that this was my three-minute seminar answer to their problems, and without actually doing a housecall it was impossible to be certain of the cause of the behavior. Both owners understood that, but at least they felt they now had a possible solution that made sense.

Follow Up

With seminars, I don't always get the opportunity to follow up on how my recommendations work out, so I was thrilled when I heard from both Peggy Bosh and Cole Anderson.

In a letter to me, Peggy wrote that the carpet scrap method worked like a charm. She admitted that she felt foolish doing it at first and, initially, Oscar looked at her suspiciously as if knowing it must be a setup.

During the first two days Oscar had a few accidents because Peggy forgot to latch the bathroom door and he got out. After six days of confinement though, Oscar used his litter-box as if he'd been doing so all of his life.

Cole Anderson phoned me four days after the seminar to say that it must've been the sand litter that Winsome needed because she used it immediately and went through the ritual of covering afterward.

"Does she still perch on the edge of the box?" I asked.

"No," he answered. "She goes right in the middle now."

Cole contacted me again after he removed the plastic sheets from the carpet and reported that Winsome showed no interest in it other than when she had a hairball to throw up. I told Cole to always make sure he has a good supply of enzyme cleaner for the carpet and a hairball gel medication for Winsome.

CHAPTER TWO

Tooth and Nail—Aggression

Being an author on feline behavior, I get numerous calls to do interviews. While I certainly welcome the opportunity to promote my books, I also look forward to helping the many frustrated owners who have questions. In addition to the frequent questions about litter- box problems, I always get asked, "why does my cat bite?"

Aggression is such a complex problem. When answering these questions, I always recommend that the owner first consult a vet, and then, if no medical cause is determined, contact a behaviorist. A truly aggressive cat is dangerous. The sudden realization that at some point your little purring ball of fluff will mysteriously transform into a cat from a Stephen King novel is terrifying. But, often, owners label their cats aggressive and mean, when in fact, they aren't.

Aggression requires you to put aside your subjectivity and look at the situation through your cat's eyes. Is your cat truly aggressive across the board? Or, is she acting aggressively under certain conditions? There are many types of aggression—can you isolate which one your cat displays? Is she showing fear aggression, say, at the vet's office? Or is she showing play aggression when she gets too carried away during playtime? Does she get aggressive toward you whenever she sees another cat outside the window? She may be exhibiting redirected aggression. There are several other types of aggressive behaviors, but I think you get my point. Determining if you're dealing with a truly aggressive cat, or a cat exhibiting aggression under certain conditions is crucial to solving the problem.

If your cat exhibits any aggression, to prevent injury, fear, and more stress, always talk to your vet. S/he will then be able to direct you to a behaviorist if necessary. Aggressive behavior shouldn't automatically result in a death sentence for a cat. Identifying the cause of the behavior and using the correct modification methods (maybe in combination with drug therapy) are crucial for success.

Some aggression cases are very sensitive because both the cat and the family are in crisis. There are times when the family has become so frightened of the cat that even if I'm able to solve the aggressive behavior, I then have to work with the family to reestablish their trust of the pet. More often though, the aggression is a case of miscommunication, meaning the owner doesn't understand what the cat is feeling, and thus misreads warning signs.

Too Hot Espresso

Miscommunication was a big part of the problem that Barry Turner and his cat Espresso were experiencing.

Barry called me to help with what he described as his cat's very aggressive behavior. It seemed that Espresso, Barry's much-loved Havana Brown, had become consistently aggressive toward anyone who entered the house. When Espresso was alone with Barry, he was loving and gentle, but toward any and all guests, he became a growling, hissing creature who would unexpectedly sink his sizable canine teeth into the closest hunk of human flesh. Do I sound a bit dramatic? Well, realize that Espresso so terrorized Barry's friends that they would no longer come over until they'd been assured that the "Evil Espresso" was safely locked in the bedroom. Barry's social life steadily plummeted. Having a girlfriend over to the house was out of the question. Even Barry's parents and younger sister refused to visit unless Espresso was incarcerated. It was strongly suggested that Barry get rid of his cat.

Despite the ridicule and criticism that Barry was receiving from everyone, he refused to give Espresso up. Even though he certainly wasn't pleased with the cat's behavior, they'd been together since Barry bought him from a breeder two years ago when Espresso was 16 weeks old.

When Barry phoned me, he'd already taken Espresso to the vet and was told the aggression had no medical cause.

With many of my aggressive cases, I prefer to fax or deliver a questionnaire for the owner to fill out and return to me before our appointment. The questionnaire is very detailed and it gives the owner time to calmly give me the details of the cat's recent behavior. It also gives me time to decide which method I should use in the consultation. The information the client gives me also determines whether it would be better to have the cat in another room when I enter. The information on the questionnaire may moreover help me decide whether to do the housecall during the day or in the evening.

I faxed a questionnaire to Barry just after our phone conversation. The completed pages were faxed back to me later that evening. The answers on the questionnaire provided valuable clues as to why Espresso's behavior had changed. Before going on the housecall, I had a good idea about where the problem originated.

A red flag went up when I read that Barry had moved twice since getting Espresso. The first move happened three months after he brought the cat home. He was waiting for his new house to be completed and the lease had expired on his apartment. A temporary move was made to a friend's home. There, Barry and Espresso had the run of the house but shared the space with Barry's friend, wife, two children (boys, aged 7 and 9), and two very opinionated Yorkshire terriers. In the behavior questionnaire, Barry admitted that Espresso spent most of the four months under the bed or in the closet. With all the construction on the new house taking up most of Barry's free time and attention, Espresso was pretty much on his own.

I made myself a note to ask Barry if Espresso had had any confrontations with the children or the dogs. Apparently, after four months, the new house was completed and Barry brought Espresso to his future home.

Regarding Espresso's aggression, Barry wrote that it shocked him because all of his friends had been crazy about the cat when he lived in the apartment. Each person greeted Espresso when they came into Barry's home and he was always the recipient of much petting. He was such a friendly kitten that many of Barry's friends loved to hold him and sought him out whenever they visited. Of course, that quickly changed when Espresso's personality took such an ugly turn.

When I called Barry to arrange a time for our consultation he assured me that Espresso would be locked up prior to my visit.

"I don't want him locked up," I replied.

"What?" Barry responded with shock.

"Just let him go normally about his day. Don't worry about how he'll react to me."

Barry was silent. He wasn't convinced that I was serious, or maybe even sane.

"Barry?" I said into the silent phone.

"Are you sure you want him loose? What if he attacks?" he asked.

"I've been doing this a long time. I can handle myself with Espresso, believe me. Anyway, I don't think he'll go after me." I assured him but I knew my words provided zero comfort.

Now I know that as you're reading this you're probably wondering why I wanted a cat loose who has a history of attacking visitors. Wouldn't it be safer to have him tucked away in another room? Would Espresso jump me when I walked in the door? Hopefully not. I was counting on the fact that I know how to enter a cat's territory without appearing sufficiently threatening to cause an aggressive reaction.

Based on the history Barry provided, I had a strong suspicion as to the cause of the problem. If correct, how I behaved upon entering the house and the way Espresso reacted to me would serve as the first behavior modification lesson for Barry (and for his cat).

I arrived at the house at the appointed time and rang the bell. Within seconds the door was barely cracked open.

"Hello, it's Pam," I whispered into the inch of darkness.

"He's loose," came a voice from the other side of the door.

"That's okay," I assured him. "The longer we stand here this way, the more upset he's liable to become."

With that, Barry surrendered his guard and opened the door. I stepped inside, just as the door was quickly shut behind me. Barry, an attractive man somewhere in his mid-30s stood before me, dressed in jeans and a crisp white shirt. Though he was trying to smile, his face had that all too familiar look of frustration that troubled cat owners get. His eyes kept scanning the room, looking for signs of his attack cat.

"Let's sit down," I suggested, motioning toward the sofa along the nearby wall. Nodding in reluctant agreement, Barry led me into the living room. Before sitting down, he took one last look around for Espresso.

The cat finally appeared just as we sat down. Espresso, a spectacular looking cat with a deep rich, chocolate coat, glared at me from across the room, but made no move other than blinking his expressive eyes. He remained that way for several minutes.

We three held our positions for a good ten minutes, then Barry watched in disbelief as his cat sauntered over toward me and began sniffing my shoes. He then moved on to inspect my purse and briefcase. Suddenly, the Kitty Tease toy that lay nearby on the carpet caught his eye. He tentatively pawed at it while periodically keeping an eye on me. I made no move to pick up the toy to play with him. I wanted him to take as long as he needed to evaluate the situation.

"He's never this calm," Barry said quietly, without taking his eyes off of Espresso. Temporarily satisfied with his investigation, Espresso retreated out of sight, presumably to the bedroom.

For a cat who normally would've been aggressive toward a visitor, his behavior was just what I'd been hoping for. And how I helped him achieve it was no magic trick—I simply let him take control over his territory. This seemed to be something he'd been unable to do of late.

The move Barry had made to his friend's house was a rough transition for Espresso. He lost his familiar territory and, to top it off, his new surroundings posed many threats. First, the territory was totally unfamiliar. The task that lay ahead for him to mark and identify what was his, was overwhelming and ultimately impossible under the circumstances. Second, the home included two children, something Espresso had never been exposed to before. From

Barry's description of life at his friend's house, the kids were used to the frantic chase games that they enjoyed with their two dogs. When Espresso came on the scene, the boys chased him, thinking he'd enjoy it as much as the dogs (though I wonder just how much the Yorkies actually enjoyed the game). When the boys weren't chasing Espresso or hunting him down, the dogs were letting him know that he wasn't welcome in their home. Espresso became reclusive, preferring to hide in the closet of Barry's bedroom. At night he'd venture out but Barry said he'd slink along the baseboards with eyes as big as saucers.

I asked Barry if he'd ever tried to explain to his friend's family that Espresso was frightened by all that was going on. He answered yes, he had tried, but when his suggestions weren't met with positive reactions, he knew he'd better not push the issue since he still needed a place to stay. He'd hoped Espresso would be able to endure the terrible conditions until the new house was ready.

What Barry didn't realize was that by that time, Espresso had become jumpy and defensive. The move to yet another unfamiliar place sent him into hiding for a week. The unpacking of boxes that Barry was doing and the related chaos kept Espresso huddled in the back of the closet, exiting only long enough to eat and use his litter- box.

Barry made many attempts to coax his cat out, and on several occasions was successful at eliciting a positive response. Barry was hopeful. Perhaps life would get back to normal soon.

Two days later, Espresso was walking around the house, curiously checking everything out. Barry's hope continued to soar. By the end of the week, Espresso seemed to be his old self again.

The following weekend, Barry's best friend was coming over to help him set up his stereo system. Danny had been over to Barry's old apartment before and had gotten along great with Espresso. When Danny rang the doorbell, Barry threw open the door and they greeted each other in their usual boisterous way, followed by playful jabs to each other's expanded waistlines. Danny caught a glimpse of Espresso and walked toward him with his arms outstretched. He liked Barry's cat because Espresso was the kind of cat who liked to pal around with you. Reaching down to scoop Espresso up in his arms, Danny was suddenly met with what sounded like a war cry and a frenzy of teeth and claws.

A trip to the emergency room was needed to treat the deep bites. Everyone, particularly Espresso, was in shock over the traumatic episode.

Upon returning to the house, Barry found Espresso back in the closet. Even though the cat had badly injured his friend, Barry did nothing to reprimand him. Instead, he blamed himself for putting Espresso through so many upheavals in his short life. Not underestimating the dangerous event that had occurred earlier, Barry left Espresso alone and went to bed. In the morning he planned to call the vet.

Barry awoke to a purring Espresso curled up next to his pillow, nuzzling his neck. By the time Barry had showered and dressed for work, it was evident to him that his cat was himself again. Whatever had triggered his aggression last night seemed well in the past, so Barry decided not to phone the vet. Maybe the worst was over. It wasn't!

The second incident happened when Barry's parents came for a visit. This time the attack was directed toward Barry's mother as she reached down to give Espresso an affectionate scratch under his chin. The injuries inflicted weren't serious but the scare it gave everyone was. As was the case after the first aggressive episode, Espresso hid in the closet, then reappeared in the morning, acting relaxed and happy.

A trip to the vet revealed Espresso to be in fine health. A prescription for Valium was dispensed, and home Barry and his cat went, hoping to get on with life again.

Two weeks on Valium did little to control Espresso's aggression toward visitors. He had successfully managed to corner Barry's new girlfriend in the bathroom. Her screams brought Barry racing to her aid, where he found her standing on the toilet, batting at a hissing Espresso with a towel.

A few more similar episodes convinced Barry that if he didn't keep Espresso incarcerated he would have no friends left at all.

Was Espresso doomed to being locked up forever? Would Barry ever be able to have a normal social life? Should Barry follow everyone's advice and have Espresso euthanized? Was Espresso truly an attack cat? Barry looked at me as if I held the answers to his whole future. It was obvious how much he loved his cat and the toll Espresso's behavior was taking on him.

After listening to his story, I closed my notebook and paused for a few seconds to collect my thoughts. Smiling at Barry, I said that if he was patient, and if he followed the treatment plan I was about to lay out, he stood a chance of getting things back to normal. Barry's face lit up. I continued, telling him that it was impossible to guarantee positive results but we had a lot on our side to work with—namely, Espresso's relationship with Barry. It was still strong and we could use that to build on. Barry sat forward in his seat, anxious to begin. As if on cue, Espresso appeared from around the corner, cocking an ear in my direction. Caught your interest, didn't I, Espresso, I thought to myself as the cat casually entered the room, looking every bit the eavesdropper.

Treatment Plan

I felt that Espresso's aggressive behavior was due to his feeling a lack of control over his own territory in his previous home, and having been under constant attack there. In Barry's friend's house, Espresso didn't have a chance to define any territory for himself. He was immediately barraged with dogs, children, strangers, and totally unfamiliar surroundings. His daily concern was his own safety with Barry's presence his only source of comfort.

The move to the new house caused Espresso to adjust to yet another totally unfamiliar surrounding. Once he realized he was basically by himself there, I think he began to overcompensate when people came over. In other words, the best defense is a good offense. Unsuspecting visitors would go right over to the cat, unaware that he needed adjustment time to evaluate and investigate who was entering his territory. That's why I've always held the theory that cats take to people who are either allergic to them or not interested in them. That type of visitor in the home will just sit on the sofa and ignore the cat. This gives the cat time to get a closer look without worrying about being grabbed. Scent is very important to a cat, so imagine how crucial it is for a cat dealing with territorial issues to be able to inch closer at his own pace in order to investigate. He may decide you're okay and become very friendly, but if you rush him before he's reached his comfort level, he'll feel threatened. That's why I was pretty sure that Espresso wouldn't attack me when I made the housecall. I gave him total control in his territory. I posed no threat.

To help take the edge off of Espresso's attitude and to help him be a bit more receptive to behavior modification, I spoke to Barry's vet about a change in his medication. I'm not a big fan of Valium for cats and especially not when it comes to aggression. I felt that the drug Amitriptyline would be more appropriate in Espresso's case. An antidepressant, Amitriptyline can have a positive effect on aggressive behavior. While there are several drugs available that are used to treat feline aggression, each case is individual and I felt that this drug would work best to disintegrate the rather large chip that Espresso had on his furry little shoulder. The drug therapy would be temporary, used just long enough to give us an upper hand when it came to the behavior modification.

Basically, Barry's assignment was to help Espresso regain his sense of territorial security. First on the list would be daily play-therapy sessions, conducted in all areas of the house. I wanted Espresso to associate positive things with every inch of his territory. The bulk of the sessions should be conducted in the living room and include the entry foyer just inside the front door. This area represented the most threat to Espresso and held the most negative association, so we needed to turn that around. Using interactive toys, Barry could allow the confident predator to come out in Espresso.

The next step was to bring someone into the house in a non-threatening way. This person would sit quietly on the sofa, allowing Espresso to take control. Barry was to keep the interactive toy handy in case diversion was needed. The principle of the exercise was to let Espresso gradually feel less threatened.

Since Espresso responded positively to me, I volunteered to be the "visitor" the first few times to Barry's home. If all went well, we would then include one of Barry's friends. I would still be there as the bridge between the familiar and the frightening.

Turning to environmental issues (Espresso's, not the world's), we needed to make the living room a less threatening, more cat-friendly place. I suggested that Barry purchase a multi-tiered cat tree and place it near the window. This would serve as a great perch to view the outside world, and would be Espresso's own personal piece of furniture. The cat tree, as opposed to the sofa and chairs, would have Espresso's own comforting scent. This way, if he felt apprehensive about a visitor but was still curious, he could safely stay in the room on his own tree—a territory within a territory.

Follow Up

Espresso began the Amitriptyline and Barry faithfully followed the play-therapy schedule. Espresso responded to the playtime with the enthusiasm of a kitten. At first, he looked around, presumably looking for signs of danger, i.e., the Yorkies or the children, but as soon as he realized that the "prey" was his and his alone, a whole new world opened up to him—life was actually fun.

Barry purchased two cat trees, one for the living room and one for the bedroom. Espresso wasted no time in claiming them.

My visits were well received by Espresso. I was able to eventually initiate play, using his favorite interactive toy. After the game, Espresso stayed close to me by stretching out on the far end of the sofa—quite a big step for him.

After two weeks, Barry asked one of his friends to join me during a visit. The answer was no. Barry asked another friend. Again, no. Espresso's reputation was well known. I asked one of my friends, someone very familiar with my methods and who knew I wouldn't put him in a dangerous situation. My friend had specific instructions on what his demeanor should be. Espresso responded favorably.

Ten months after my last visit, the report from Barry was glowing. Espresso, weaned off the Amitriptyline two months after my initial housecall, has been friendly and sociable to strangers. To avoid any potential threats and to allow his cat adequate investigation time, Barry always requests that all guests not approach Espresso, rather allow him to come to them.

By the way, Barry wanted to make sure I let you know that his social life is great now. Espresso likes his girlfriend and the future is looking good.

The Raccoon Incident

Redirected aggression is a term used by behaviorists to describe a common form of seemingly unprovoked aggression. A cat displaying redirected aggression can take his frustrations out on another pet, or a member of the family.

To help you identify what redirected aggression is, imagine driving in a car under terribly stressful conditions (snowstorm, heavy rain, etc.) with your spouse in the passenger seat. Your knuckles are white against the steering wheel and you're tense and frightened. Suddenly your spouse says something or offers a suggestion about the way you're driving. Under such tense circumstances you snap at him or her with a verbal onslaught of not-so-nice expletives. Your spouse isn't the cause of your agitation but he or she becomes the redirected target.

The most common example of redirected aggression among companion cats is when there is the sudden appearance of a strange cat in the yard. For instance, two companion cats who have peacefully lived in the same house are sitting by the window, watching the birds. Suddenly, an unfamiliar cat appears in the front yard. The two cats looking out the window become very nervous. One of the cats begins to growl, then in a flash he lashes out at his buddy, teeth and claws bared. If you're lucky, the confused cats recover from this crisis relatively quickly. If you're not so lucky, or if the original source of the problem continues to cause agitation, then the relationship between the companion cats deteriorates.

In my experience, I've found that if the cats are separated immediately after the incident, there's a good chance that all will be forgotten by the next morning. Unfortunately, in many of the cases I've been called to treat, the cats were left together where they would remain agitated with one another. Long after the true trouble source has left the yard in search of other cats to terrorize, the two hapless companions remain at odds with each other.

Such was the case with Pebbles and Bam-Bam, two domestic short-haired cats. The two were littermates that had been rescued at the age of five weeks by Roger Beresford. Mr. Beresford, a confirmed bachelor at the age of 62, had been sharing his quiet life with Pebbles and Bam-Bam (given those names by his niece) for the past ten years. The two cats were inseparable, often sleeping so tangled up together that Mr. Beresford found it impossible to tell where one cat left off and the other began.

Peace and harmony came to a crashing halt one evening when an uninvited raccoon began working a small hole in the screen on the kitchen door. Bam-Bam was having a little snack at the food dish, when he turned and saw the raccoon on the other side of the door. Bam-Bam's loud meow sent the raccoon scrambling away and brought Mr. Beresford running from the living room to see what was going on. Pebbles tiptoed in behind her owner, curiously peering from behind his leg.

Bam-Bam, with tail puffed, inched toward the kitchen door, growling and hissing. Not having ever seen her brother act that way before, Pebbles delicately walked over to him and was instantly pounced upon in a frenzied attack. Within seconds, Pebbles flew from the room with Bam-Bam in hot pursuit, a hunk of Pebbles' fur trapped in the corner of his mouth.

Two months after that incident I was called because things had gone from bad to worse. As I sat in Mr. Beresford's living room with pictures of his cats on nearby end tables, I listened to his story. He had tried everything, he said. Whenever he caught Bam-Bam stalking Pebbles he would squirt him with water or clap his hands. Now it was at the point where they could barely be in the same room together.

"If things don't improve, I'll have to give one of the cats away," Mr. Beresford said as his eyes remained fixed on Bam-Bam, who lay grooming himself on a nearby overstuffed chair.

"Pebbles was unfortunately in the wrong place at the wrong time," I began, "and because Bam-Bam was so agitated, he redirected his aggression to the closest target. When cats aren't separated shortly after such a traumatic episode like the one you've described, the tension can remain quite high between them. As a result, each cat is no longer acting the way the other is used to, and they are becoming defensive toward each other. As time goes by, the original cause of the problem (i.e., the raccoon) isn't even a factor. From each cat's point of view, the other cat is now a threat."

Mr. Beresford ran his slender fingers through his gray hair and then scratched his chin absentmindedly. He attempted a smile before he spoke. "You may think I'm a sentimental old man, but I love these two cats. Men aren't supposed to like cats, are they?" He asked, leaning forward in his chair as if sharing a secret with me. "They've been my best friends so let's do what it takes to get them back to normal."

"We'll give it our best shot," I answered. His expression changed from one of worry to a look of determination. It was time to get down to work.

Since Bam-Bam hated the very sight of Pebbles, and Pebbles fled at the first hint of him being anywhere in the vicinity, we'd have to use bribery, diversion, positive reinforcement, and a good dose of luck in order to gain some ground.

In spending time with Bam-Bam, I found him to be playful and responsive. After some initial suspicion directed toward me (something I'm very used to), I was able to engage him in some play, using an interactive toy. Knowing that he could be easily manipulated through the use of a toy would be of vital importance when we eventually brought Pebbles back on the scene.

Next, I tracked Pebbles down in her owner's bedroom, and attempted to do a play session with her. While not as responsive as Bam-Bam, her curiosity did eventually get the best of her, so I knew that if Mr. Beresford worked at it, he could get her to play.

In my tour of the house, I found one litter- box that both cats had shared in the past without a problem. Even though Mr. Beresford reported that there had been no spraying or urinating outside of the box, he did inform me that Bam-Bam would wait outside the bathroom door whenever he heard Pebbles scratching around in the litter. When she jumped out of the box, he'd pounce on her, causing her to run back to the master bedroom, her sanctuary. I told Mr. Beresford that he was lucky, because from what he described, a litter-box problem was very close to surfacing. Being under a constant threat, and having only one option when it came to the litter- box, could soon drive Pebbles to seek safer, more secluded areas. Just to be on the safe side, I took my black light and searched the whole house for urine stains but found nothing.

After spending time with the cats and viewing the layout of the house, I felt I could map out a plan for Mr. Beresford. I wanted to try using behavior modification first, without the aid of drug therapy. But if needed, I would talk to Mr. Beresford's veterinarian about putting one or both of the cats on medication.

As we went back into the living room and took our seats, I explained in detail to Mr. Beresford how redirected aggression works and how the intense feelings from that one traumatic episode had now snowballed into constant day-to-day tension. We needed to help each of his cats stop viewing each other as an immediate threat. Once we accomplished this, we could begin to rebuild the relationship. I was unsure at this point if we could get Pebbles and Bam-Bam back to the relationship they had previous to the raccoon trauma, but we'd take it a step at a time. Any improvement over the current state of affairs would be most appreciated by Mr. Beresford.

Treatment Plan

Step number one involved giving each cat some breathing room. Pebbles didn't need to live in fear every time she had to use the litterbox, and Bam-Bam didn't need to feel that his very existence was threatened by having another cat in the same house. I wanted each cat to feel a little relief, so I asked Mr. Beresford to separate them for a few days. While they were separated, a second litter box would be set up for Pebbles in the master bathroom, just off of the bedroom. Mr. Beresford said he didn't mind the extra box, especially if it meant less trauma for Pebbles.

"Even after we reintroduce the cats," I explained, "having a second box will take a little of the pressure off. This way, if Bam-Bam is guarding one litter box, or if he's actually in the box, Pebbles has the option of using the second one."

Very often, I've found that in multi-cat homes, whenever there is just one box, and especially if the path to the box is narrow (i.e., a hallway leading to the bathroom), it can be very intimidating for the submissive cat.

Next on the list was the boosting of the self-confidence of each cat. Yes, I know that sounds silly, but it helps. The way I do it is through good old-fashioned play therapy and positive association. Since we can't sit the cats down and have a heart-to-heart chat with them about how there's no reason to feel threatened and that they each have rights in this territory, we have to convey it in a language that they'll understand. What I've found in my years of behavior counseling is to use what nature has already provided. I look at a cat for what he is—a predator. It makes sense to me that if a cat is a successful predator, he becomes a confident cat. If he's not good at hunting and is frightened by every sound he hears in the woods, then not only will he starve to death, but he'll become an easy target for every bully that passes by.

Treatment Plan (continued)

My plan was for Mr. Beresford to do individual play therapy with each cat several times a day. To create total safety and to prevent one cat from becoming distracted by the appearance of the other cat, when doing individual sessions, he was to make sure the second cat was kept out of the room. We certainly didn't want Bam-Bam charging in on a session with Pebbles. That certainly wouldn't do much for confidence building, now would it? So the first step with individual play therapy is to allow the cat to see she or he is completely safe. Initially, Pebbles might be distracted because she'd be expecting Bam-Bam to bulldoze through the room. Eventually, as she realizes that he's not around, and as the prey (interactive toy) becomes just too inviting to resist, she'll begin to make attempts at stalking it. With each session she'll become more the predator and less the timid victim. These sessions allow her to have some time when she's not under stress, and will also provide positive associations with certain areas of the house. Initially, the play therapy should be done where she feels the most secure, probably the master bedroom, but eventually the sessions should extend to other areas of the house.

For Bam-Bam, these sessions would help redirect some of his negative energy into something positive. They would also allow him to feel confident by making him feel like a successful hunter, without trying to bully Pebbles.

An additional way to boost confidence during play-therapy sessions is to place boxes or open paper bags in the middle of the room. Since cats like to hide behind trees, bushes, and rocks as they inch closer to their prey, Mr. Beresford would need to provide adequate cover for his hunter. For a nervous or timid cat such as Pebbles, allowing her to hide behind a box in the middle of the room would help her to venture away from the furniture and the walls. She would be so distracted in her pursuit of the toy, she wouldn't realize that she had just expanded her comfort zone.

I went over all the specifics of play therapy for Mr. Beresford. It was important that he not make the mistake that many owners make when playing with their cat: causing frustration. I wanted him to move the interactive toy as if it were prey so that his cats would respond as predators. I didn't want him to constantly wave the toy around, causing the cats to be frantic in their attempts to capture it. Our goal wasn't kitty aerobics. I wanted each cat to have time to plan, stalk, and achieve numerous victories. Keeping the toy out of reach, or just keeping it in constant motion wouldn't give Pebbles or Bam-Bam adequate time to go through all of the natural mental and physical preparations. In Pebbles' case, it was crucial that she be provided enough time to stalk and plan because she needed to feel that the capturing of prey was well within her ability.

Another important part of the play therapy would be the way in which Mr. Beresford ended each session. Just pulling the toy away from Pebbles or Bam-Bam and walking away would leave them wondering what the heck happened to the prey. They might still be charged up and in need of a longer session. What I wanted Mr. Beresford to do was to simulate the movement of prey that was getting weaker or beginning to die. I told him to view it as he would any exercise: a warmup, intense exercise, and then cooldown. The cooldown during the last couple of minutes in play therapy would allow his cats to feel that they had actually conquered their prey, and would hopefully leave them a little more relaxed.

All that Mr. Beresford had to do was to move the toy at a slower rate. For instance, if he was using a bird-like toy with feathers, he would eventually move it as if the bird had a broken wing, was getting weaker, or unable to fly anymore. He would then let Pebbles or Bam-Bam have one grand finale capture.

The next way in which Mr. Beresford would use interactive toys would be for diversion. I explained that when he reintroduced the cats he needed to keep an interactive toy with him that could be concealed from them. For example, the Cat Dancer can be wound up and easily carried discreetly from room to room. Whenever he saw even a hint that Bam-Bam was about to bother Pebbles, he was to divert his attention to the toy. The point was to break the pattern of Bam-Bam immediately going after Pebbles. By using the interactive toy, Mr. Beresford would be diverting his cat's attention with something positive. Bam-Bam would much rather go after prey than chase Pebbles. In this way, a negative situation would be turned into a positive one. At the same time, Pebbles would see that when Bam-Bam entered the room, it didn't always mean he was going to attack her.

The third stage of play therapy would involve group play. It would take some coordination on Mr. Beresford's part, but if he could hold a toy in each hand, he could conduct a group session with both cats. The purpose of doing the group session with two toys was so that one cat didn't get bullied or shut out. I wanted each cat to see that they could have a good time and feel safe with the other cat in the room. They would be playing together in a sense, but they'd only be aware of each other out of the corner of their eyes. I stressed to Mr. Beresford that under no circumstances was he to conduct a group session with only one toy. Pebbles would inevitably feel threatened and retreat back to the bedroom.

Now for the bribery part of the behavior modification plan. Bribery works, and I'm not ashamed to say I use it any time I can. All it involves is using a small treat that both cats find impossible to pass up and giving it to them when both are present. For example, it can be a small commercial treat tidbit, a teaspoon of yogurt, a morsel of cooked chicken, whatever the cats will go crazy for. By dispensing it only when both cats are present, they will continue to associate good things with each other. Eventually, Mr. Beresford can allow them to enjoy their treats when they are closer to each other. However, I warned him not to rush things and attempt to feed them too close together. It would be better not to risk a setback.

After dispensing a few other minor instructions, I left Mr. Beresford's house feeling confident that he'd do whatever it took to bring peace back to his home. I told him to call me in a week with a progress report. At that point I would decide whether to speak to his vet about medication.

Follow Up

Mr. Beresford followed my instructions to the letter and soon became adept at conducting play therapy sessions that were nothing short of feline fantasies. The diversion therapy worked well in that it managed to distract Bam-Bam away from Pebbles every time: he became much more interested in the potential capture of prey than in antagonizing Pebbles. At first, Pebbles played it safe and ran from the room as soon as she saw Bam-Bam. Eventually, with the help of her own individual play therapy and good old faithful bribery, she began to stay in her position and watch with a very cautious eye.

Two weeks into therapy, Mr. Beresford left the message on my answering machine that I'd been hoping for. He said that when Bam-Bam walked in the room, Pebbles raised her head up, looked at him for a moment, and then went back to sleep on the overstuffed chair. I smiled as I listened to the message, knowing that there might still be some setbacks ahead, but we were definitely on the right road.

The bribery part of the therapy proved to be nothing short of a miracle. Whenever Mr. Beresford brought out the treats, both cats raced toward him. Within a month, they were rubbing up against one another as their owner opened the package and placed a treat in front of each of them.

One year after my visit, life in the Beresford household has remained peaceful and happy. Mr. Beresford continues to do daily play-therapy sessions for the benefit of each cat, and he says that it has become a special time for the three of them. Group play sessions are a nightly ritual.

Having gone through the experience of redirected aggression with Bam-Bam, Mr. Beresford has become more alert to the potential of a repeat crisis. He reported to me that one day he saw a stray cat sitting on his deck. Before he could chase him away, Bam-Bam caught sight of him and began hissing. Mr. Beresford immediately whisked Pebbles off to the bedroom to keep her from experiencing Bam-Bam's redirected wrath. He then shut the blinds to the sliding glass door, got out the package of treats and shook the container, something he said always brings Bam-Bam running from wherever he is. Bam-Bam didn't break tradition and came out, winding himself around Mr. Beresford's legs and purring. After the treat Mr. Beresford played with Bam-Bam. When he had conquered his prey and was ready for a nap by the fireplace, Mr. Beresford crept into the bedroom and played with Pebbles. Later that evening he opened the door to the bedroom and Pebbles walked back out to the general part of the house. When Bam-Bam saw her, he greeted her in the way that had now become a pattern: sniffing her pretty little face and then licking her ears.

The most rewarding part of the behavior modification came when Mr. Beresford called to say that he saw his two cats once again sleeping together in the curled up position that they used to enjoy before the raccoon incident.

Family Counseling

The phone number displayed on my pager belonged to one of the animal hospitals in town. The "911" following the phone number indicated the urgency of the page. On my way home from my last client of the day, I returned the call from my car phone and was immediately put through to one of the technicians.

"Dr. Fields is in the exam room," the tech said in a rush of words. "He asked me to call you because a married couple is here with a cat for vaccinations and the cat has scratched the wife several times. They aren't bad scratches but the cat's going bonkers in there and so are the owners—the wife is yelling at the husband. Dr. Fields finally managed to grab the cat and had Dr. Whitson do the vaccs," the technician finally took a breath before going on. As I listened, I turned my car around and headed for the animal hospital. The tech continued her report, "The wife wants the cat put down. The husband refuses to do it. Pam, it's bad in there. Dr. Fields needs you. Is there any chance that you can get here?"

"I'm headed your way now. I'll be there in about 10 minutes," I said, hoping there'd be no traffic surprises.

When I arrived at the clinic I was greeted by Cindy, the head technician, who ushered me right into the back lab area. "Dr. Fields wants to talk to you first," she said and then disappeared through a door to an exam room.

I stood at the lab counter watching the bustle of activity as several techs darted in and out of rooms. I was remembering my years as a tech and how exhausted I'd be at the end of the day, when suddenly the exam room door opened. Dr. Fields gave a half-hearted wave as he walked toward me.

"Hi, Pam, I'm sorry to do this to you," he said quietly as he leaned his back against the counter, crossed his arms over his chest, and let out a heavy sigh. He was an exceptionally tall man with broad shoulders, thick arms, and large hands. He towered over all of the staff and often looked awkward when handling tiny puppies or kittens. "The cat freaked out in there. The owners brought him in for vaccinations and nobody could get him out of the carrier. We finally had to dismantle the crate but by that time the cat was going nuts." Dr. Fields unfolded his arms from across his chest and I noticed tiny red spots on the front of his jacket where his arms had been resting. I looked down at his hands and saw several long scratches. He noticed where my eyes were directed and held out his hands in front of him. "Ebony managed to tag everyone," he said.

"What do you want me to do?" I asked as I glanced toward the door to the eerily quiet exam room.

"Apparently, according to Mrs. Stanley, the cat has been showing more aggression at home, and after this episode she doesn't want the cat anymore. He has become increasingly more aggressive each time he's been here. We've seen him for abscesses from cat fights, once for castration surgery, a couple of ear infections, and the usual vaccinations."

"As with most animals, the only experiences they associate with the vet's office are painful ones," I responded.

Dr. Fields nodded. "But the husband loves this cat and refuses to do anything. He thinks the cat is aggressive because the wife hates him."

"Do they want a consultation?" I asked, not looking forward to working with a couple on opposite ends of the cat tolerance scale.

"They don't even know that I called you. I feel that there's nothing wrong with the cat. He just hates coming here. I don't know why he's become aggressive at home. His physical exam checks out normal. We can handle an aggressive cat here at the hospital; it's what's happening between the husband and wife that worries me. You have much more experience with this kind of thing." He put his hand on my shoulder and I have to admit that for a brief second my thought went to my new jacket and I hoped he wasn't getting any blood on it. "You can take as long as you need," he offered. "The exam room is yours."

"Thanks," I said with just a hint of insincerity as we walked into the room.

Dr. Fields introduced me and explained why he'd called me for help. Then he started out the door, saying he'd be with a patient if we needed him.

When the door closed, I looked back at Mr. and Mrs. Stanley and smiled. They were each on opposite ends of the room. I was greeted in return with a hopeful smile by Mr. Stanley. Mrs. Stanley, on the other hand was, well, let's just say that her side of the room was a bit frosty.

The blue plastic carrier sat on the floor between them. From where I stood, the only thing I could see was a dark shadow inside.

Even though everyone in the room was now relatively calm—*tense*, but calm—signs of the recent battle were everywhere. Black cat hair was all over the table, and there were little black puffs rolling on the floor, pushed around by the sudden burst of air from the floor registers. Two thick white towels lay heaped in the corner. The large amount of black hairs all over them were evidence of their recent use as shields against claws and teeth.

A pair of scissors, a roll of gauze, and a bottle of peroxide lay on the counter near the sink, sure signs that somebody had either been bitten or scratched. Mrs. Stanley's hand was wrapped with a couple layers of gauze. Having had many cat scratches myself, I empathized with her.

"I know this has been a very emotional and stressful experience for all three of you," I began. "I'd like to offer my help if you're willing. Maybe together, we can figure out a direction to go from here."

"Put the cat to sleep," Mrs. Stanley stated quietly. Her voice was still a bit nervous from her recent trauma. "He changes too much, especially when we have to bring him here. He sees that cat case and we have a hell of a time getting him inside. Jim has to throw a blanket over him and dump him in the case."

Mr. Stanley reached down and pulled the blue carrier closer to his side of the room, almost as if his wife's very words could carry out a death sentence. "He's only like that when he sees this case. He knows he's going to the vet and he hates it. I can't blame him," he spoke in defense of the silent dark shadow in the carrier at his feet.

"How do you explain his biting me at home?" Mrs. Stanley asked her husband.

I walked over to the counter and pulled the stool out. As I sat, I pointed to the chairs along the wall. "Please sit. May we talk for a few minutes? I might be able to offer another perspective."

Mr. Stanley looked over at his wife. "Come on Judith, you're talking about *killing* my cat. Can't we at least discuss it together?" Mrs. Stanley reluctantly walked over to the chair and sat down. Her husband took his place next to her, then we began.

I asked them questions about how they got Ebony, how he behaved at home and specifically, how they each interacted with him.

Ebony was the only pet in the Stanley home. He had wandered up to their back door over a year ago. Despite Mrs. Stanley's reservations, they adopted him, and he became an indoor/outdoor cat who spent a lot of time outside with Mr. Stanley as he worked in the yard. Retired, Mr. Stanley loved puttering in the garage or sprucing up the property. Ebony kept him company through almost every project. Mr. Stanley loved his two-year old companion. Ebony was "a man's kind of cat," as his owner described him. A black domestic shorthair with a big broad face, he was solid, muscular, and agile. "A great mouser," Mr. Stanley said proudly.

"A flea hotel," interjected Mrs. Stanley, "Plus, he bites me."

"Tell me about the biting," I asked Mrs. Stanley.

"Whenever I get out of bed or step out of the shower, he bites my ankles. And he sheds so much, oh my gosh, I'm forever chasing him with the brush but he hides. When I do catch him though, I brush and brush and get piles of hair. He hates it but I can't have all that cat hair everywhere in my house."

"He's a cat, Judith, and cats shed," said Mr. Stanley in the cat's defense.

"But he's mean too. You see what he's done," she said, pointing to her bandaged hand.

We talked some more about life in the Stanley household. A picture was developing. This wasn't an aggressive cat, but there were several different problems occurring. The problems though, had more to do with the owners than with the cat. He was just reacting to what was being dealt to him. If the Stanleys were willing to let me (and I knew Mr. Stanley would be), I felt I could shed light on their cat's behavior and effectively improve it overall.

Treatment Plan

I went through all of the specifics with the Stanleys, starting with Ebony's fear aggression at the vet's office. The way the Stanleys described how they always herded Ebony into the carrier and that the carrier was only brought out to go to the dreaded vet, meant they were pumping him up with fear right from the start. He knew he was in store for something bad when that awful carrier appeared and then his beloved owner started chasing him and throwing a blanket on him.

I advised the Stanleys to take some of the fear out of the appearance of the carrier by leaving it out all of the time. Putting a towel inside and leaving the carrier open in a corner of a room would get Ebony used to seeing it. I told them to place a small treat a few inches in front of the carrier. If Ebony responded to that then the next day they could put the treat right in front of the carrier. They were to slowly work the treats inside so that Ebony would see that he could come and go freely.

I explained to the Stanleys another important reason to be able to get their cat in a carrier without too much trouble. In an emergency, if you have to leave your home quickly (for example, a fire), being able to get the cat in the carrier will mean a safer exit with no chance of him jumping out of your arms.

Treatment Plan (continued)

Next, my plan was to help cut down on the amount of stress that Ebony has to endure at the vet. I learned from Mr. Stanley that they'd had a long wait in the waiting room that night, surrounded by dogs and other cats. We needed to reduce this type of added anxiety which can get a cat worked up before he even gets into the exam room. I suggested that they make their appointments as early as possible (before things start getting backed up) and to wait with Ebony in the car. Apparently, once they'd loaded him in the carrier he settled down during the ride. His agitation began after being in the waiting room for 20 minutes. Being able to bring him right in would eliminate that huge build-up of fear.

I also felt that neither Mr. Stanley nor the technician should spend time in the exam room trying to yank the cat out of the carrier. With Ebony, I felt the quicker and more efficiently things went, the less he'd get agitated. My advice was to have the vet and the tech disassemble the top, quickly restrain the cat (always using the minimal amount of restraint needed), do the exam and administer the vaccinations. Apparently, in the past, the hospital staff had tried cat muzzles, restraint bags, etc., all of which caused Ebony to struggle more and become more anxious. There seemed to be a window of opportunity with him before he became aggressive, and I was hoping they wouldn't spend that precious time trying all of these other methods.

Then I recommended that after Ebony became comfortable with the carrier that they take him on small car trips around the block, down the street, etc. After returning home he was to be given a treat. I wanted him to see that not every ride ended with a painful time at the vet. I also wanted them to bring Ebony to the vet occasionally for no medical reason at all. Just a "hello" visit so he'd see that every trip to the vet didn't always mean bad things. They weren't to stay long though. My reasoning for wanting to desensitize

Ebony to the veterinarian's office was that he'd had abscesses from cat fights, he was young (2 years), and would probably be at the vet many times in his life. Apparently he was a fighter and Mrs. Stanley wasn't willing to keep him strictly indoors, so sadly, there'd most likely be more abscesses in his future. He needed to become a cat that the staff could handle and medicate more easily.

I explained that the so-called "aggressive" behavior that Ebony was displaying at home by biting at Mrs. Stanley's ankles and feet was play aggression. Basically, he was in play mode and the sudden appearance of feet in motion was too irresistible to pass up. Upon delving further into the story, I discovered that the biting occurred when Ebony was kept in the house for long periods. He loved to hunt and play outside, often stalking and pouncing on leaves and twigs. When outside with Mr. Stanley, Ebony was frequently treated to lots of playtime. Unfortunately, Mr. Stanley used his fingers to entice and tease the cat. He even admitted that at night, when stretched out on his recliner, Mr. Stanley would wiggle his toes and Ebony would attack in play.

Whenever the weather was cold or rainy, Ebony chose not to go outside but he'd often pace inside, going from room to room. Mr. Stanley would be out in the garage and Mrs. Stanley would be in the house. It was at those times that Ebony would attack her feet.

I explained to them that by using fingers as toys, Ebony was taught that it was permissible to bite skin. Add to that, the abrupt decline in playtime on the days when the cat stayed inside the house. He had a high energy level, enjoyed being a mouser, and was improvising by attacking Mrs. Stanley's ankles. The solution for the problem involved a change in the way Mr. Stanley played with Ebony. From now on it was to involve interactive toys. When outside, if Ebony wanted to pounce on a leaf or a flower, that was fine, but Mr. Stanley wasn't to use his hands even if he did wear gloves. (Mr. Stanley had tried to negotiate with me.)

Treatment Plan (continued)

I showed Mrs. Stanley how the use of interactive play would eliminate Ebony's biting at her feet. I also explained how to set up things in the house to make indoor life a bit more interesting. She could leave a ping-pong ball in a box or throw a light, fuzzy toy, or the plastic ring from the milk jug on the floor for Ebony to bat around when she didn't have time to play with him.

Setting up a cat tree near a window (Ebony wasn't allowed on the furniture) would give the cat something to climb on and provide a great vantage point for checking out the birds.

Adding to Ebony's attitude problem was the way in which he was chased down and tortured during grooming. I didn't blame him for running every time he saw Mrs. Stanley coming at him with a brush. So we went over a new approach to grooming that would help him actually like the process. Mrs. Stanley rolled her eyes in disbelief, but I pressed on anyway.

Ebony was to be brushed by Mr. Stanley for a while. The brushing would consist of one or two light strokes down the back. That's it! Mrs. Stanley argued that the cat hair would build up and be on everything but I explained that we were retraining Ebony to change his view on grooming. We needed to go slowly. The purpose of the exercise was to have it be over before he realized what had happened. One or two strokes of the brush, followed by a pat or a scratch under the chin. Gradually, they could increase the number of strokes, but the key was to finish before Ebony became uncomfortable. By having Mr. Stanley do the grooming initially, Ebony would hopefully break the negative associations with Mrs. Stanley, the brush, and images of torture. I wanted Mrs. Stanley to be associated only with positive things (i.e., playtime, feeding). This gradual reintroduction to grooming would help Ebony accept handling better so he would eventually be able to tolerate ear and teeth cleaning, nail trimming, etc.

When I had finished all of my recommendations, I asked Mrs. Stanley if she'd be willing to try any of this before giving up on Ebony, because the cat meant so much to her husband. At least trying behavior modification would show him that she was willing to find the best solution. Mrs. Stanley's face softened when I said this. I felt that appealing to her relationship with her husband was the route to go instead of trying to explain how dreadful it is to euthanize a perfectly healthy cat. My hunch worked, and she agreed to try things my way.

I gave them my card with instructions to call me any time.

Follow Up

By leaving the carrier out and placing treats inside, Ebony eventually became very comfortable with its presence. He even began using it for naps.

Ebony now accepts and even welcomes grooming. It took a while and there were several messages on my answering machine from Mrs. Stanley about cat hair, but it did finally work. Mrs. Stanley said that Ebony purrs now when being brushed. They've come a long way.

The gradual desensitization of the veterinarian's office worked well. The Stanleys said that they felt foolish driving their cat to the vet to say "Hello," but it ultimately helped Ebony become easier to handle. This proved very timely because eight months after I met the Stanleys, Ebony developed an eye infection. Dr. Fields reported that he was much easier to handle and that nobody got so much as a scratch.

The play aggression biting has ceased since Mr. Stanley no longer uses his fingers to tease and instead uses the interactive toys.

And, finally, by doing play sessions with Ebony, Mrs. Stanley's heart has warmed up to the black cat. One night when Ebony and Mr. Stanley were in the recliner, the cat got up out of his lap and settled next to Mrs. Stanley on the sofa.

Additional Notes

To hopefully avoid potential aggression problems at the vet's office, if you have a kitten, try periodically bringing him in for "Hello" visits. It has been my experience that the staff of nearly every vet welcomes these visits and understands their importance.

If you have a cat who is extremely aggressive at the vet, changing the type of carrier that you transport her in can make the visit less dangerous for all concerned. For truly aggressive cats, I've found that top loading carriers work best. With this type of carrier, when the tech or vet opens it up, they have a better angle to get hold of the cat securely and safely (usually by holding the scruff of the neck with one hand and the hind legs with the other). The quicker the restraint, the less the cat struggles and his stress level won't soar off the scale. The top loading carriers also make it easier and safer to put the cat back inside.

Another common mistake that people make when choosing carriers is that they pick one that is too large. The bigger the carrier, the more difficult it will be for you to carry and your cat will end up being jostled around as she slides from one end to the other. Feeling the walls of the carrier around her also creates a sense of security for the cat and makes her feel like she's in a good hiding spot. You've seen what small boxes and bags cats will crawl into—they prefer to feel the security of having the walls surround them.

Additional options for cats who are too aggressive at the veterinarian's office is to ask the vet about the use of a mild tranquilizer. If you're able to medicate your cat at home, your vet can prescribe medication that might just take the edge off of your cat's panic. If you feel your cat is at the point where she needs medication, speak with your vet.

Finally, some cats who show aggression at the vet's do much better when the vet comes to the house. Most veterinarians do housecalls, and many cities have mobile vet services.

CHAPTER THREE

Cats as Interior Decorators—
Furniture Scratching

Anyone who has a cat that scratches furniture can tell you how frustrating it can be. It's the kind of behavior that causes cats to be endlessly punished, declawed, given away, banished to the outdoors, or euthanized.

Owners try everything to get their cats to stop scratching the furniture. And therein lies the problem. They're trying to get their cats to *stop* doing something that the cat knows he *should* be doing.

To a cat, scratching is as natural as hunting a mouse, grooming herself after a meal, purring, meowing…oh heck, it's as natural as *breathing*. Scratching serves many vital functions for a cat. It conditions the claws by removing the outer dead nail sheath; it leaves a visual mark (remember, cats are territorial); it also leaves an olfactory mark due to the scent glands in the cat's paw pads.

Another less obvious (but certainly no less important) benefit of being able to scratch is that it serves as an emotional outlet.

You may notice that the time your cat chooses to scratch the furniture is when you walk in the door after being gone all day, or while he's anxiously watching you prepare his dinner.

Being able to scratch is such an important aspect of a cat's physical and emotional health, that I hate to see owners misunderstand their cats' intentions by labeling them as willfully destructive.

I couldn't include a chapter on scratching without touching on the subject of declawing. It is, and probably will always be a sensitive and controversial topic among cat owners. There are those who feel it's nothing short of a barbaric procedure to subject a cat to declawing surgery. There are those who feel that once the paws have healed, declawed cats are unaware that their claws are even gone. They continue to scratch furniture, only without the damaging effects. Now the two camps—for and against declawing, aren't made up of unfeeling cat haters on one side and fanatical cat worshippers on the other. We're talking about vets, behaviorists, cat experts, and owners. Because there are so many educated, professional, and informed people out there who share such opposing views on declawing, I feel the subject will remain up for debate for a long, long time.

My view on the subject is that it's truly an inhumane, unnecessary procedure. I base that opinion on my years as a behaviorist, having worked on numerous occasions to successfully train cats to use scratching posts. It's also based on my years in a veterinary hospital, attending to the cats coming out of anesthesia after declawing surgery. I've watched them wake up banging themselves against the cages, in a manner unlike recoveries from other surgeries. I've held cats whose paws were so painful that they were unable to even sit up to eat or use the litter box.

Imagine having the first joint of all of your fingers amputated and then having to use your hands. Sounds painful, huh?

Having said that, I assure you there are ways to train your cat to a scratching post. Not all posts are alike though. Some are great and some aren't even good enough for firewood. For a scratching post to be a success, it must meet four requirements:

1. *Sturdiness*
2. *Proper height*
3. *Appealing material*
4. *Good location*

Many scratching posts fail on all four points. Let's look at them individually.

STURDINESS

Go to a pet supply store and handle the scratching posts. Put your hand on the top and try to wiggle the post. Many times it wobbles and is poorly connected to the base. How is a cat supposed to lean on that and scratch without the fear of it toppling over? That's one reason why she chooses your sofa or a chair. She knows that thing isn't going anywhere. Choose a post that's well constructed with a wide, heavy base. You may have to pay more, but it's far less expensive than buying new furniture.

PROPER HEIGHT

When your kitten was three months old, the post you bought was great. He could not only scratch on it, he could climb up, down, and all over the thing. But, as he grew, a funny thing happened— the post didn't grow with him. If you happen to have a tall cat (as I do), when he reaches up for a full stretch he covers a lot of ground. Maybe that's why the tall back of the sofa is where he chooses to scratch. He knows he can get a good stretch.

Appealing Material

Choosing a post that's covered with carpet is an open invitation for furniture destruction. The carpet-covered posts are too soft and make it difficult for a cat to scratch effectively.

The better choices may not *look* as appealing to you but they'll *feel* more appealing to your cat. Any rough material that enables a cat to really sink his claws in will keep him returning to the post. Sisal-covered posts or any rough and tough material will do. Even bare wood makes a great scratching surface. Just think *rough*.

Making your own post isn't as hard as you might think and it enables you to customize it to your cat's requirements (i.e., height and choice of covering material). To make a basic post, screw or nail a 4x4 piece of wood to a flat, heavy wooden base. Determine the height of the post based on your cat's approximate length during a full stretch. For the base, make it wide enough so the post won't topple over when your cat leans on it. For very tall posts, make the base wide enough for your cat to put his hind feet on it for extra stabilization.

Cover the post with any appealing material. I chose to wrap rope around mine that I secured at the top and bottom with heavy staples. When it gets too worn out I just unwrap the rope and replace with a new one. You can cover the base with any kind of carpet or just leave it bare.

GOOD LOCATION

Putting a great scratching post in a lousy location will guarantee noncompliance from your cat. Spend a little extra time noticing *where* and *when* your cat scratches and place the post in response to those needs. For example, a cat who loves to stretch and scratch after a nap should have a post near her favorite sleeping area.

My cats have three posts in three different locations to accommodate their preferences. I have one cat who always scratches after eating and post-meal grooming. That post is located near the food bowl. My other cat loves an intense stretch and scratch session after a nap. She also prefers to sleep in an elevated spot. I purchased a multi-tiered cat tree with the pole supports wrapped in rope. Olive now sleeps on the top of the tree and then jumps down to use the built in scratching post after nap time.

My third post is near the front door to allow my cats to express their joy at the arrival of myself and my husband at the end of the day. After greeting us they run over to the post and scratch.

All I did was watch my cats' patterns and I came up with a solution that pleased all of us. They get to scratch, and I get to keep my furniture intact.

Be as creative as you need to be when it comes to planning your cat's scratching post. Don't skimp on anything or you'll be throwing out your favorite chair because it's beyond repair.

Verticals and Horizontals

While at a fund-raiser one evening, a veterinarian came over and introduced himself to me. His practice was about 40 miles outside of Nashville. We'd spoken many times on the phone and he had sent me numerous referrals over the years but we'd never met. I was standing in line for the buffet, talking to friends when I saw this gentleman come rushing toward me.

"Pam, it's easy to pick you out in a crowd," he began, "because I've seen you so many times on TV. The clients I've sent to you have all come back with positive reports."

As the man continued to speak, his voice sounded very familiar and I tried to discreetly glance over at his name tag because I didn't have the slightest idea who he was. When I read the name I felt my face flush as confusion turned to recognition. Having spoken to this veterinarian on the phone at least 20 times over the last few years, I'd developed a mental picture of him. I remember thinking that over the phone his voice was so distinctive and appealing. The richness of his tone mixed with the quiet way in which he spoke made me wonder how many of his female clients had difficulty paying attention to his instructions or got lost in the sound of the voice. I pictured him to be tall, incredibly handsome, and well built. I pictured dark hair just beginning to gray at the temples, Paul Newman blue eyes, and an engaging smile.

Well, so much for my ability to match the voice to the face. Let's just say that the man standing before me was lucky if he stood over five feet in shoes. I'm sure he must've had hair at some point in his life (and it may even have been dark), but there was hardly a trace of it now. His temples were graying but then again that was the only place on his head where there was actually any hair. And while he did have blue eyes, Paul Newman certainly didn't have anything to worry about.

"If you have a minute, could I talk shop with you?" He asked.

We formally introduced ourselves and as we both stood in line for the buffet, he asked me about a client of his, one whom he had called me about several months earlier.

The client, a woman in her late 30s, had a 9-year old male cat who had been tearing up her furniture for most of his life. Apparently, the owner's attempts at training had consistently failed to the point where she eventually gave up and just surrendered the furniture to the cat.

Dr. Biondi had first called me concerning this client when she had come to him to discuss having her cat declawed. It seemed that she had recently gotten married and Michael, her new husband, didn't want the furniture that he had brought into the marriage, to get destroyed (a reasonable request). Since his sofa and living room chairs were in far better condition than hers, they got rid of her damaged furniture.

Andrea Calloway told Dr. Biondi that within hours, Rudy had scratched the sofa. In a panic, Andrea tried to cover it by tossing a few pillows on the sofa with the explanation that they added a decorative touch. Rudy though was just getting warmed up. He was born to scratch and now he had all this unmarked furniture in front of him. Michael's sofa and chairs soon resembled their predecessors.

Dr. Biondi tried to discourage Andrea from declawing her 9-year old cat. He asked if she had a scratching post for him and she replied that she had them all over the house but Rudy totally ignored them.

Andrea and Michael Calloway wanted to buy new furniture but knew it was impossible as long as Rudy had claws. Time was running out for Rudy because Michael, who was not as attached to him as Andrea, wasn't as tolerant of his destructive tendencies. The cat had to be declawed or else he'd be restricted to the outdoors. Andrea was beside herself because Rudy had been an inside cat from the time she first brought him home. It started when she saw some teenagers standing outside the supermarket with a box of kittens. Andrea passed them by, not sure that she even liked cats. She walked into the store, did her shopping, and walked out, stopping at the teenagers' box only long enough to notice that there were just two kittens left. They were cute, she thought, but it was not the right time for a pet.

By the time Andrea had driven home and unloaded her groceries, she realized she'd been thinking about the one gray-striped kitten. There'd been a solid gray one left also but there was something about that striped one. Andrea put her jacket back on, grabbed her keys, and headed back to the supermarket. If the striped one is there, she thought to herself, it's meant to be. If he's gone, I'll just go back home.

When Andrea pulled up alongside the supermarket entrance she noticed the teenagers walking in the parking lot with the empty box. All the cats were gone. It's strange, she thought, she actually felt disappointed. She hoped the gray-striped kitten found a good home.

Just as Andrea was about to drive off, she noticed a little girl and her mother walking very briskly toward the teenagers. In the mother's hands was a kitten. Which kitten was it? Andrea strained to see. As the mother handed the kitten over to one of the teenage boys, Andrea saw that it was in fact the gray-striped kitten. The mother took the little girl's hand and walked away. The stern look on the mother's face led Andrea to believe that the little girl had taken it upon herself to adopt the kitten without permission. Mom apparently didn't share her daughter's enthusiasm.

Andrea put the car in drive and pulled up to the teens. "Are you still giving away that kitten?" She asked.

"Yeah, sure," one of the boys answered, obviously surprised at his sudden good fortune. "Our mom said we had to find homes for them. We thought we'd gotten rid of them all, but then that girl's mom made her bring it back." He smiled at Andrea and held the kitten out to her. The kitten squirmed and wiggled to get free of his grasp. "You want it?"

"Is it healthy? How old is it?" Andrea asked, knowing that she was already falling in love with the kitten and health or age was irrelevant.

"It's, ah, I think 7 or 8 weeks old. And yeah, it's healthy. Come on, it's free, what more do you want?" replied the impatient teen.

Andrea reached through the open window and took the kitten from the boy. The kitten appeared to be shivering and the damp, cold November air wasn't helping. She unzipped her jacket, placed the kitten inside and zipped it back up. "That'll keep you warm until we get home," she said to the kitten as it tickled her neck.

On the way home, Andrea stopped at the pet store and stocked up on supplies for her new friend: food, bowls, litter, litter box, toys, and a scratching post.

Nine years and several unused scratching posts later, Andrea was now faced with a decision: her cat or her husband. Michael was becoming increasingly intolerant of Rudy's habits and felt Andrea's lack of training success indicated that it was time to seek a more permanent solution: declaw the cat or keep him outdoors.

When Dr. Biondi first called me regarding Andrea's cat, I asked him to find out what kind of scratching posts she had purchased. I recommended that she try the Felix Post (1-800-24-FELIX), a scratching post that I've had repeated success with over the years. I also told him to recommend that the post be put right next to the sofa. The sofa and chairs were to be covered with strips of double-faced masking tape or completely covered with a sheet, making sure all ends were tucked in securely.

I instructed Dr. Biondi to give Andrea my usual speech about not punishing her cat for scratching the sofa, but instead, rewarding him when he uses the post. I felt that a change to a better post would make a difference, and Andrea would see positive results soon.

A week later I received another call from Dr. Biondi. Andrea had purchased the scratching post I'd recommended and covered the furniture as per my instructions. Not only had Rudy continued to ignore the post, he'd now begun to scratch on the carpet—something he hadn't done before. Declaw surgery was scheduled for the following week.

I was *not* happy! "Uh, oh," I said. "It sounds like we have a *horizontal* scratcher. That's what the problem has been all these years. I'd better talk with her." It took some convincing but Dr. Biondi finally got Andrea to agree to a housecall.

Once there, I realized why Andrea's husband had been so upset. Freddie Kreuger couldn't have done a better job at slicing and shredding the furniture.

Rudy, having been disciplined repeatedly in his life for scratching, knew better than to even be in the same room with his owner. The relationship between Andrea and her cat had deteriorated to such a point that he avoided her altogether. I had a lot of work to do in order to repair the emotional damage.

The damage to the sofa and chairs was just as I'd expected. The back and side of the furniture remained untouched. All the damage was confined to the tops and all along the cushions. Rudy was indeed a horizontal scratcher. That's why all of the scratching posts weren't of interest to him. They were all *vertical*.

Of course, at first Andrea thought I was crazy when I began talking of horizontals and verticals but it began to make sense as she looked closely at her furniture and at the newly damaged carpet.

"Most cats scratch on vertical surfaces," I explained. "For instance, out in the wild a cat would probably scratch on a tree. That's why we simulate the tree indoors with a scratching post. There are also many cats who do both horizontal and vertical scratching, perhaps because it stretches their muscles in a different way. Some cats scratch horizontally strictly out of preference for a particular material. For instance, they may prefer the rough texture of the welcome mat so they alter their scratching technique to be able to have access to the best surface."

I went on to explain that there are also those few cats who, for whatever reason, just prefer a horizontal scratch over a vertical one. Based on the evidence before us, Rudy was obviously one of those cats.

"So we don't have to declaw him?" she asked hopefully.

"No, I don't think you'll have to declaw him," I answered. "We just have to turn your verticals into horizontals."

Treatment Plan

There are several inexpensive scratching pads available at pet supply stores. They're made of corrugated cardboard (something cats find very appealing for scratching). The pads come in various shapes and sizes. Many are treated with catnip for added enticement. I wanted Andrea to buy a few of these and place them next to the furniture. The sofa and chairs were to remain covered for the time being.

Since Rudy had been reprimanded so often for scratching, I instructed Andrea on how to use an interactive toy with him to ease any hesitation. Playing on and around the scratching pads would also guarantee a claw or two finding its way into the cardboard. Once Rudy experienced the feeling of the cardboard, especially during the excitement of playtime, he'd want more. As he realized he was no longer being punished for scratching, he'd eventually become more relaxed, and the relationship between Andrea and Rudy would begin to repair itself. Daily play therapy done by both Andrea and Michael would also do wonders to get the family back on track emotionally. Andrea was not to purchase any new furniture until Rudy's scratching habits were solidly directed toward the pads.

Treatment Plan *(continued)*

Andrea already had a Felix Post in the house, one with an incredibly appealing cover material. I suggested that she place it on its side so Rudy could scratch it horizontally. She could do that also with all of the posts in the house. Sometimes with horizontal scratchers, you can eventually stand one of the posts back up vertically, and the cat will continue to scratch on it. After nine years of horizontal scratching, I wasn't sure that Rudy would be open for something new, but I told Andrea she should give it a try.

Follow Up

Rudy never kept his declaw surgery appointment and will never need to make another such appointment. All it took was to notice the consistent pattern to his scratching and to come up with a solution that satisfied both cat and owner.

Using your imagination is sometimes the best way to solve a behavior problem. Not all cats read the manual on how to be the typical cat, so that means you may have to look for a not-so-typical solution. There's always one out there, you just have to find it—sometimes it's horizontal, sometimes it's vertical.

Why Spray When You Can Scratch

Theresa Alvin thought she had her cat figured out. Conway, a 7-year old, ruddy Somali had been the perfect cat. He was playful, affectionate, and friendly to all of Theresa's guests, and he never misbehaved.

Originally from Chicago where they lived in a high-rise apartment, Theresa and her cat moved to Nashville, where she was finally able to buy a home of her own. Divorced for 15 years, Theresa at 53 wanted to be near her first love, country music. With her family spread all over the country, she figured it wouldn't matter where she lived and decided it was time to fulfill her dream.

Conway seemed exceptionally happy with his new location. The house provided lots of room to play and hide. Having windows that looked out on a yard opened up a whole new world for the 7-year old cat who'd seen nothing but sky and clouds previously. He spent hours watching the birds in the trees and remained fascinated with leaves that tumbled across the lawn in the breeze. Theresa was thrilled to watch her cat enjoying life so much. She even put up a birdbath in the backyard to add to Conway's entertainment. He loved it.

In addition to cardinals, blue jays, and other birds, the birdbath unfortunately drew other, less welcome visitors to Theresa's backyard, namely the neighborhood cats. It was when she heard a banging at the window that Theresa first saw how popular her birdbath was with the local felines. She came running from the bedroom to find Conway standing up on his hind feet, slapping at the window with one of his front paws. Theresa got to the window just in time to see a big orange cat running from the yard with a bird in his mouth. Two other cats were sitting near the birdbath, waiting for their opportunity to catch lunch. "I'm sorry, Conway," she said. "I think I'll have to get rid of the birdbath." The next day, Theresa sadly dismantled the birdbath and put it away in her garage. As she walked back toward the house, she caught a glimpse of Conway watching her from the window, which made her feel even worse.

With the birdbath gone, Theresa thought her problem with the neighbor cats was over. Well, for *her* it was, but for *Conway* the memory was a bit more difficult to shake. Theresa first began to notice a problem when she found Conway running over to the window, turning his back to it, and getting into a spraying stance. So far, all he did was a lot of tail twitching and meowing, but Theresa knew it wasn't a good sign.

First thing in the morning Theresa hauled her cat off to the vet just to be certain he wasn't having a bout of LUTD (Lower Urinary Tract Disease). After Conway received a clean bill of health, Theresa brought him back home, relieved that he wasn't sick, but worried that he might be on the verge of exhibiting some unpleasant behavior.

For the next week, Conway continued to back up to the window and twitch his tail but so far he hadn't sprayed. He was making Theresa nervous. "If you're going to do it, will you just get it over with and stop torturing me," she said to her startled cat one night after watching him twitch his tail for what seemed like the 30th time. Conway's only response was a throaty meow. "I can't stand it any longer," Theresa told the vet over the phone the next morning. She was given my number.

During our initial telephone conversation I instructed Theresa to block Conway's view from that window. I suggested she tape cardboard over the bottom of the window so Conway couldn't see out to the backyard. My next suggestion was to place one or two bowls of food along the wall beneath the window to reestablish that area as a *nest* and not a perimeter in need of marking.

Before ending our conversation I told Theresa to use diversion in the form of play therapy to lure Conway away from the window, and hopefully to break the behavior pattern he'd been demonstrating. She thanked me and agreed to call in a few days with an update. If these suggestions didn't work, I'd set up a housecall.

Three days later Theresa called and said Conway was hanging around the window less but was still periodically backing up to the wall and twitching his tail. I agreed to come over.

Now I know you're thinking this story shouldn't be in the chapter on scratching, but it turns out that it had more to do with scratching than with spraying. I include this story to show you how important it is to look at the cat's entire environment and not focus narrowly on the immediate problem area. You'll see what I mean as you read on.

During my housecall I found Conway to be restless. His mock spraying seemed to occur whenever he was unsure where to direct his energy. The move to the new house certainly opened up a whole new world for him, but it also created new anxieties. For some reason (and Theresa was indeed lucky) Conway was at this point content with just going through the spraying motions without actually spraying.

As I went through Theresa's house with my black light (just to be certain that Conway hadn't actually made good on his threat to spray), I noticed that the cat didn't have a scratching post. I remembered Theresa saying that her cat hadn't been declawed, so maybe I'd just missed it when I toured the house.

When I asked Theresa about the absence of a scratching post she said that Conway had never seemed to need one.

"And he has never scratched the furniture?" I asked.

"Not that I've ever seen," she replied.

Treatment Plan

Based on Conway's restlessness and his need (however subtle) to mark, I wanted to try an experiment. I wanted to put a scratching post near the window. I had two reasons. First, I thought he might be satisfied to mark his territory by scratching (remember that scratching

Treatment Plan (continued)

leaves both a visual mark and a scent mark). Next, since scratching can be a displacement behavior, I thought it might provide him with a more positive emotional outlet. In addition to a standard scratching post, I suggested that Theresa get a cat tree that Conway could climb as another energy-releasing activity.

When Conway lived in the high-rise apartment there was less to stimulate him. In the new house, he was exposed to more exciting things and was trying to come up with appropriate reactions.

Theresa was instructed to conduct daily play-therapy sessions with Conway to help direct his energy and restlessness toward something positive.

Follow Up

The addition of the scratching post and cat tree provided Conway with the outlet he needed. He transferred his desire to mark that had manifested itself into backing up to walls and tail twitching, to happily scratching on his post. Whenever his energy started getting the best of him, he zoomed up and down his cat tree which served as a signal for Theresa that it was time for a play-therapy session.

A few days after getting the scratching post and cat tree, Theresa removed the food bowls from along the wall. The cardboard was removed from the windows two weeks later.

Conway now uses his post whenever he sees a strange cat outside. He no longer exhibits any tail twitching no matter how much potential anxiety the outdoor scene may contain.

What's Mine Is Mine

What do you do if you have the most stubborn cat on the planet? What else is left after you've tried every kind of scratching post? What do you do when your cat still thumbs her little nose at her post? Horizontal, vertical, rope, carpet, bare wood—nothing works. Your cat still insists on clawing things she shouldn't.

I experienced such a cat when I met Hannah, the 2-year old calico owned by Donna and Rick Catalano. Hannah was the most recent addition to a household that already included three other cats.

Rick had rescued Hannah two months earlier when he found her nearly frozen to death underneath his car in the driveway. It was a frigid night and the temperature had dropped rapidly. Rick was outside trying to cover as many of the shrubs as possible. That's when he saw the skinny cat peeking out from behind the front tire. When he walked toward her she was too weak to even run away. Rick took a blanket off one of the shrubs and wrapped it around the frightened cat. He then brought her inside the house and placed her in one of the extra bathrooms. He lined a small cardboard box with plastic, and filled it with litter. He then searched through the kitchen cabinets for a couple of small dishes and filled one with water and the other with canned cat food. When he saw that she was too weak to eat, he took his finger and hand-fed her.

When Donna came home from her night out with the girls and noticed her three cats camped out in front of the bathroom she knew something was up. No one ever used that bathroom because the pipes made such an awful sound every time you turned on the faucet. So what was going on, she wondered.

"Rick?" she called out tentatively to the closed door. "Are you in there?" She looked down at her three cats. All of them remained fully alert, eyes fixed on the door. Something was up. "Rick?"

"Guess what we have," came Rick's voice from the other side of the door.

"Don't tell me there's a cat in there," she replied. Judging from her cats' reactions there had to be some kind of animal in there.

Silence.

"Rick?" she called again and leaned her ear against the door.

"Well, okay, I won't tell you then."

Donna straightened up away from the door. "Rick, do you or do you not have a cat in there?" she asked again, only this time more sternly.

"Well, you said not to tell you," came his reply. Donna wasn't amused.

Two months and several vet visits later, a healthier Hannah was now an official member of the Catalano family. The other three cats appeared to handle the change with a minimum of complaints. A confident trio, they let Hannah know right away that they were in charge. Hannah accepted her position in the family and within a short time, hisses, growls, and paw slaps were few and far between.

In a multi-cat household there has to be a pecking order. Even if there are only two cats, one will emerge as the more dominant of the pair. It may be reflected in behavior such as who gets the choice sleeping area or who gets access to the food bowl first. Whenever you increase the number of cats, it's expected that there'll be some adjustment period as the newcomer learns what territories belong to the higher-ups.

What I find interesting about the little territories (i.e., the sofa, the cat tree, the big overstuffed chair, the bed, etc.) is that the cat who claims the territory may be different depending on the time of day. For example, the cat who must always sleep in the top perch of the cat tree during the day may have a different territory for the evening. This means another cat can claim the cat tree at night. As long as all cats are in agreement on the scheduled sharing of territories, this feline version of musical chairs helps maintain harmony in the household. Sometimes, though, there are a few places that are not, and never will be, negotiable. Hannah soon found that out.

Donna and Rick called me to their house to figure out if there was any way they could train Hannah to use a scratching post. The three other cats used scratching posts but Hannah chose to scratch on doors, walls, even the brick fireplace hearth. As much as they didn't want to declaw her, if Hannah didn't change her ways, Rick and Donna were going to do it. Since all of the cats enjoyed an indoor/outdoor existence, that would mean confining Hannah inside.

During the housecall I asked Rick and Donna if they'd ever seen Hannah use a post, even just once? "In the very beginning she did," answered Rick, "but she'd get chased away by one of the other cats. They weren't used to her being in the house yet."

In my tour of the house I saw three well-worn scratching posts and three cardboard scratching pads. Donna said that up until they got Hannah, their cats had never damaged anything in the house. They had all taken to the posts immediately.

Looking at the places Hannah chose for scratching I noticed they all seemed to be in *neutral* areas, meaning places that didn't seem to be of territorial concern to the other cats. For instance, Hannah scratched the doors in the upstairs hallway, the closet door near the front door, the fireplace hearth, and the smallest of the living room walls in which the only furniture was an accent table. She also scratched on the wallpaper in the dining room, and even on the legs of one of the chairs. It was the one chair, Rick said, that none of the other cats used. The other three chairs had cushions that Donna had made but she hadn't gotten around to completing the one for the fourth chair.

As I toured the house I began to see that the three cats had long ago established ownership of the six scratching posts, and they remained quite territorial after Hannah arrived. In questioning

Rick and Donna further, they started to recall seeing particular cats routinely going to specific posts. By the time Hannah came onto the scene, no one was willing to share. After being chased enough by the other cats, Hannah got the message and decided to find alternative places to scratch.

Treatment Plan

Since Donna and Rick didn't purchase a new post when they first took in Hannah, I suggested they do so now. In order to help her identify with it and to let the other cats know that this one was hers, I suggested that they pre-scent it with Hannah's own scent. To do this, one of them was to put a pair of socks on their hands and rub Hannah all over, especially concentrating around her scent glands (cheeks, paw pads, top of the head). Once they'd given her a good rubdown, they were to distribute that scent on the new scratching post by rubbing it all over with the socks. During the first week they were to freshen the scent by performing the sock rubdown on Hannah and rubbing the post with the socks every day.

Part two of the plan was to have play sessions with Hannah around the post using an interactive toy.

To discourage Hannah from going back to her behavior pattern of wall scratching, Rick and Donna were to cover the scratched areas by taping long sheets of paper on the walls. Strips of double-faced masking tape were to be affixed to the paper. The sticky paper would be removed only after we were sure Hannah's scratching habits were firmly redirected toward the post.

Follow Up

Having a post that didn't already carry all the scents of the other cats made it easier for Hannah to feel comfortable using it. The sock rub-down accelerated it becoming her own personal territory. She now scratches on her post and shows no interest in the walls, hearth, or furniture.

Within two weeks, the paper had gradually been removed from the walls.

As the cardboard scratching pads have become completely worn out, Rick has slowly replaced them. In the process, Hannah has had the opportunity to scratch on them. With the new cardboard pads the cats are willing to scratch cooperatively, but they remain individually attached to their vertical scratching posts.

CHAPTER FOUR

Behaviors They Never Warned You About

There are those of you cat owners who have the good fortune not to experience any behavior problem more unusual than how to keep the cat from jumping on the counter. Then there are those of you who, well, who are given a little extra challenge in life. It's to you that I say, keep your sense of humor, remember the love you have for your cat, and no matter what all the neighbors tell you, *you don't have the cat from hell.*

Fascinating Faucets

It's not unheard of for a cat to develop a fascination or obsession with a particular item. It could be a spot on the wall that your cat never gives up on, forever believing it to be an elusive bug. Some cats become fascinated with certain movements on TV. My cat is hypnotized by the cursor on my computer screen. One of my clients has a cat who guards the VCR, intently watching the blinking digital time display.

While such fascinating objects occupy only a small portion of a cat's busy schedule, there are those single-minded felines who relentlessly pursue the object of their obsession, almost to the point of being unaware of life around them. Spencer is a perfect example of such a cat.

Spencer, a 2-year old tortoise shell tabby, had a fascination with water. Generally, it's not uncommon for a cat to enjoy watching a dripping faucet, occasionally pawing at the water. Some cats even become fixated on their water dish and will put their paw in it or just watch the swirling movement. Then there are the cats who refuse to drink out of the water bowl at all, choosing the water running from the faucets instead. For too many owners, what began as a cute little game of laughing at your kitty as he played with the dripping water, has now become the water-on-demand syndrome—meaning, when the cat wants water, he sits by the faucet and waits for his ever-faithful owner to turn it on for him. Some cats are so lucky to have such well-trained owners!

For Spencer, merely playing with the drips from a faucet or a melting ice cube on the kitchen floor didn't satisfy him. What started out as an amusing curiosity soon crossed the line into obsession. Spencer constantly had to be around running water.

When Spencer was just a kitten, his owners, Bill and Nancy Brock, thought it was so cute the way he'd climb up their legs and sit on the kitchen counter to watch the dishes being washed.

"He'd sit on the edge of the sink and wouldn't take his eyes off the running water the whole time I washed dishes," Nancy said during our phone conversation. "Then, when he got bigger and was able to jump on the counter by himself, he'd sit next to the sink and stare at the faucet."

To amuse Spencer in between dish-washing time, Nancy would turn on the faucet so drops of water would slowly fall. This soon became the routine not only in the kitchen, but also in each bathroom.

"Bill wasn't at all happy with the dripping faucets," Nancy said, "but if we didn't keep them running, Spencer would sit by the sink and meow."

Spencer even earned the nickname "Drippy" by his owners. He lost all desire for any activity other than eating, and even that was done hastily so he could return to the faucet. He eventually began sleeping by the sink. This broke Nancy's heart because from the time he was a kitten he'd always slept between Nancy and her husband.

The Brocks, though not pleased with Spencer's obsession, were willing to tolerate it, that is, until his behavior began taking a rather frightening turn.

It began with unlatched doors. Spencer was accepting the limitation of having to be content with dripping faucets and the regularly scheduled melting ice cubes in his water bowl, but if he heard a faucet running or toilet flush (he even loved to watch the bowl as it filled with swirling water) from behind a closed door, he'd meow, claw at the door, and if it wasn't securely latched, he'd barge right in on some unsuspecting soul. Spencer had no regard for someone's privacy when it came to his water-watching needs.

During the next few months, as long as everyone securely closed the bathroom door, Spencer appeared resigned to his daily ritual of watching Nancy do the dishes. Peace in the Brock household was to be temporary though. Spencer was making plans and his obsession was about to reach a new high.

According to Nancy, it began as an ordinary day (as ordinary as life with Spencer could be). Bill had gone off to work and Nancy was washing the breakfast dishes. As usual, Spencer was stretched out by the side of the sink, supervising every drop of water as it left the faucet. Nancy finished rinsing the dishes and loaded them in the dishwasher as Spencer yawned, stretched lazily, then dozed off.

With the kitchen work done, Nancy gave her sleeping cat a light kiss on the nose, then headed to the bathroom for her morning shower.

Nancy undressed, turned on the shower and stepped in, grateful that Bill had already warmed up the bathroom from his earlier shower. A few minutes later she felt a slight draft. Nancy figured she hadn't latched the door and Spencer must've pushed it open. Feeling the chill, she readjusted the water temperature when out of the corner of her eye she noticed the shower curtain move slightly. "Must be the draft," she told herself and proceeded to shampoo her hair.

The curtain moved again. Nancy stuck her head out from the curtain to see how far open Spencer had pushed the door. She reached her arm out and pushed the door closed, noticing Spencer wasn't in sight. She ducked back in the shower, shivering from the cold.

Feeling relaxed and warmer, Nancy decided to take a longer shower than usual and even felt daring enough to sing. Midway through "I Will Always Love You," Nancy heard what sounded like a sneeze. She peeked out from the shower. "Spencer?" she called as she looked around but saw no cat.

Nancy went back to her shower and her song when she heard a second sneeze. Once again, she stuck her head out from the shower and scanned the bathroom. "Spence?"

"Meow," came the reply.

That's strange, thought Nancy. It sounded as if the meow came from behind her, *inside* the shower. She slowly turned around.

"Meow."

Sitting in the shower, directly behind Nancy was a very wet cat.

"Spencer!" Nancy screamed and threw open the curtain, jumped out and grabbed a towel, her heart beating wildly. She reached back in the shower to turn off the faucet, figuring Spencer must've bolted, but there he sat. Nancy shut off the faucet and looked at her cat who was staring up at the last few drops of water that were clinging to the shower faucet.

Now you're probably thinking that the Brocks called me after this incident to work with Spencer. Not yet. Nancy and Bill just decided to be more disciplined about keeping the bathroom door locked. They were a tolerant couple.

It wasn't until after the *second* shower incident that I was called. This incident involved Bill's mother, who was visiting for a few days.

Not being a cat lover, Elena Brock wasn't thrilled to find Spencer suddenly right next to her whenever she came close to a faucet, whether she was getting a glass of water or brushing her teeth. She'd been warned about the cat's behavior and was reluctant, but willing to tolerate it during her visit.

The second episode happened on the third day of the visit. It was early on Sunday morning and Elena was unable to sleep any longer. She got up, made coffee for herself, and read the paper. Bill and Nancy were still asleep. Even Spencer must've been sound asleep somewhere because he hadn't come by the sink when Elena ran water for her coffee. She'd thought it was odd but was grateful for the absence of the annoying cat.

Elena decided to take her shower while waiting for Bill and Nancy to wake up. She turned on the shower to warm the tub before getting inside. She'd always hated stepping into a cold tub, especially first thing in the morning.

While waiting for the water to heat up, Elena went into the guest bedroom to get her clothes and bring them back into the bathroom. Shutting the door behind her, she pulled on it twice to make sure it was securely closed. Bill had even put a sign on the door, warning guests to be sure the door is always latched. Elena mumbled to herself about how foolish her son had become over a cat.

Elena took off her robe, hung it on the hook behind the door, then removed her eyeglasses. The warm water felt good as she stepped into the shower. Closing her eyes, she let the water cover her head, when suddenly, she felt a little tickle on her right ankle. She looked down but saw nothing but the swirling water. She continued on with her shower.

She began shampooing her hair when she felt another tickle, this time on the other foot. She looked down again. For a second she thought she saw a flash of something dark by her foot, but without her glasses her eyes weren't very good.

When it happened again, Elena was certain something actually touched her foot. She looked down, squinting her eyes in an attempt to focus. Even without her glasses, and with shampoo dripping into her right eye, there was no mistaking that something had moved. She quickly turned and looked down toward the back of the tub. Nothing. Then the shower curtain on the outside of the liner began to move.

"What's going on?" an angry Elena said as she turned off the water.

The shower curtain stopped moving. Elena pushed aside the liner and peered outside the tub. That's when she came eye to eye with Spencer, who was hanging halfway up the curtain. Both of them dripping wet, they stared at each other in disbelief for a few seconds before Elena let out a scream. Spencer took that as his cue to drop from the curtain and hide behind the toilet. Elena got out of the tub, with shampoo still in her hair, to physically evict Spencer from the bathroom. Making sure he was truly locked out, she started back to her shower when she heard a worried Nancy and Bill knocking on the door. "That cat has to go," Elena huffed as she pulled the shower curtain back into place. "He's a menace."

Nancy Brock called me that afternoon on the recommendation of her veterinarian. Spencer was getting out of hand.

When I visited Nancy and Bill's house, I saw the home of two extremely busy people. The furnishings appeared more functional than decorative. The place resembled an office more than a home.

"I apologize for the house being a bit dusty," Nancy said as she attempted to fluff up the sofa pillows. "I just can't keep up on housework the way I used to."

I glanced around the living room, which was crowded with shelves filled with books. The coffee table was covered with papers, a briefcase, a laptop computer, a portable phone, and several unidentifiable candy wrappers.

Bill sat down in the chair across from me. "Nancy and I are lawyers. We work long hours both at the office and here," he said as he pushed the papers on the coffee table off to one side, revealing coffee stains and rings from probably too many long hours of late-night work.

As soon as adequate space was created on the table, Spencer made his appearance by jumping up, sitting directly in front of me and looking right into my eyes. He blinked slowly and I noticed tiny droplets of water around his head.

"You've been in the sink again, haven't you?" I asked as I reached my hand out for him to sniff.

Another slow blink was his guilty reply.

"Spencer, get off the table," scolded Bill as he pushed the cat to the floor.

After getting enough background from the Brocks, I toured the house (including all faucets) and spent time with Spencer. His obsession with water was the most extreme I'd seen. But after spending a good amount of time with him, I got the feeling that water was the only source of entertainment in that house for Spencer.

"That's nonsense," Bill said after I told him of my opinion. "He has a basket full of toys."

"But do *you* play with him?" I asked.

Bill laughed and scratched the side of his head. "We don't have any time. That's why we got a cat because they're supposed to be less trouble than a dog."

"There isn't enough stimulation for him," I said as I pointed to the toys in his basket. "All of these toys require Spencer to do too much work to make them come alive. The water dripping out of the faucet provides the movement that keeps him interested. And, as he got more comfortable being wet, he decided to go for the ultimate game...the shower. He's just following the pattern that you and Nancy set up for him."

I took Bill and Nancy on a tour of their own house so they could see it through Spencer's eyes. They saw just how uninteresting their home was for a cat. There weren't any elevated spots for perching or available access to any window. Every table was covered with stacks of books and papers. Spencer was immediately reprimanded if he attempted to land anywhere but the pre-approved counter by the sink. He was bored and lonely.

Treatment Plan

With some cases of obsessive behavior, the aid of drug therapy is required. Prozac and similar type drugs have been helpful in breaking the pattern. While I kept the option open to use such a drug if I needed to, I wanted to try a few other strategies first. I had a feeling that Spencer would respond without the aid of a drug. I felt that boredom was the root of the problem.

Treatment Plan (continued)

My plan for Spencer consisted of several strategies. First, I showed Nancy and Bill how to use interactive toys on a daily basis to entertain him.

"Fifteen minutes three times a day is what I want from you," I said as I guided them through the basic technique. "Chasing one of these toys will be much more interesting than watching water drip from a faucet."

Spencer responded to the toys with leaps, jumps, and perfectly timed pounces.

"I know you're both very busy but if you could each just set aside this small amount of time it would make a world of difference in Spencer. He needs stimulation," I pleaded as Nancy and Bill watched their cat darting happily around the room.

"We can do it," Nancy said.

The next area we had to cover was how to keep Spencer entertained during the long hours he spends alone. I suggested the possibility of a companion cat. They both agreed that it was worth a try.

"Even with another cat, you'll still need to make his house more cat friendly," I said. "A cat needs a place to perch. He feels safer off the ground. It also gives him a good vantage point to survey his territory. Spencer needs his own furniture."

I discussed getting a couple of cat trees. One should go in the living room, right in front of the large, sunny window. The other should go in the upstairs office where Nancy and Bill spend so much time. That way, Spencer could have his own spot instead of constantly being pushed off the desk.

My other suggestion was that Nancy and Bill get a fish tank to amuse Spencer.

"Since he loves to watch the movement of water, a fish tank could amuse him for hours," I said. "You'd have to make certain to get a very secure top for the tank but it could be an interesting alternative to the faucet for your cat."

"We could put it in the office upstairs," Nancy suggested. "It might have a calming effect on us when we're working. I like the idea."

Bill agreed but was concerned about when they'd find time to clean the tank. I told him to inquire at the fish store about someone to come in and maintain it.

The last thing I wanted to do was set up a little device that would serve as a water dish with a pump in it to create movement. I brought along a product called the Kitty Kreek. This water dish is made especially for cats. The pump circulates the water up to the top of the simulated rock, where it trickles down to the basin. The Kitty Kreek has helped redirect cats away from faucets. It's also useful for cats who insist on drinking from the toilet. Hopefully, the Kitty Kreek would aid in keeping Spencer off of the sink and out of the shower.

Since Nancy tended to pile the day's dishes in the sink until evening when she would rinse them off after dinner and load the dishwasher, I suggested that Bill take Spencer into the bedroom or office at that time for his play-therapy session. This would help to break the pattern of him sitting by the sink during dishwashing time.

Follow Up

The next day, in addition to purchasing some interactive toys, the Brocks went out and bought a fish tank. That night, Nancy phoned me to say that Spencer was captivated by the tank. Bill seemed pretty fascinated by it too.

A week later, the cat trees that had been ordered through a catalog had arrived. I went over to help Nancy set them up in the right spots and to entice Spencer to claim them as his own.

By the end of the week, Spencer was no longer interested in the kitchen faucet or the bathroom shower. He spent his time watching the fish in the tank, sitting on his cat tree, watching birds outside, occasionally viewing the water in the water dish, and engaging in play session with the Brocks.

Two months later I phoned Nancy to tell her I'd found a cat with a personality I felt would be compatible with Spencer. Bill and Nancy came over to meet little Ruthie. She won their hearts.

Six months have gone by and the Brock household is happy again...well, almost. The good news is that Spencer is completely over his water obsession and he and Ruthie get along beautifully. They play so much that they often scatter the papers that Nancy or Bill are working on.

The bad news is that Elena Brock won't come for overnight visits anymore (she prefers to stay at a motel) because the last time she was over she found Ruthie asleep in the tub and nearly drowned her when she went to turn on the shower. She's convinced that one can't take a shower safely in her son's home anymore. Nancy tried to explain to her that Ruthie likes to sleep in the cool tub on very hot days but Elena didn't buy the story. Actually, Nancy confessed to me that not having Bill's mother visit anymore wasn't really such bad news after all. She's not too wild about her mother-in-law.

Don't Pet Pickles

My pager was going off for the third time in seven minutes. I was in the middle of a consultation at a client's home and I normally don't answer pages during a session but I figured that unless I turned my pager off, whoever was on the other end wasn't about to give up. I excused myself, went to the telephone, and checked the display on my pager. The readout indicated that the same phone number had called three times. I picked up the phone and dialed the number, preparing myself for what was sure to be an emergency.

"Hello?" said the quivering voice on the other end.

"This is Pam Johnson Bennett returning a page," I said calmly.

"My cat won't let me into my house!" the woman screeched into the phone. "I opened the front door and he lunged at me. I tried going in the back door, and he was right there. He's turned into a lunatic. He had a wild look in his eyes." Then she took a few nervous breaths. "I can't get in my house. I called my vet, and he said to call you. Can you come right over?"

"I'm in the middle of a session right now," I replied as I glanced at my watch. "I'll be finished in about 30 minutes. I'll phone you from my car as soon as I'm through."

The woman was not pleased. "You don't understand," she answered, overenunciating her syllables for effect. "I cannot get into my house! My cat won't let me in any of the doors. I'm sitting in my neighbor's kitchen. I have groceries in the car, and I need to get into my house."

I looked back at my clients who were patiently sitting in their living room, waiting for me to return. "The best I can do is call you in about 30 minutes. I have appointments scheduled for the day but I'm going to try to get to you as soon as I can."

The woman on the other end of the phone sighed in defeat and agreed to wait for my phone call. I took down her name and address and promised I would get back to her immediately. Twenty-five minutes later, I was in my car, phoning Marion Estee, the recently banished cat owner. After receiving directions to her house, I phoned my next appointment to tell them that I would be a little late.

As I pulled into Marion's driveway, a woman came running out of the house next door, with another woman following right behind her. From the very serious look on the face of the first woman hurtling toward me, I assumed she was Marion Estee, and the second woman, with the rather amused look on her face, was her neighbor. I usually get a sinking feeling in my stomach when clients come rushing out to meet me. It never means anything good. I braced myself.

"Thank goodness, oh, thank goodness," Marion called out as she came around the front of my car and yanked open my door before I'd even turned the engine off. "Nothing like this has ever happened before. I just can't believe he's doing this." The words seemed to gush out of her mouth as she tried to lead me to the front door.

"Hold on for a minute," I said and put my arms up to prevent her from pulling me along. "Before we go in there, I need to get some background on what happened."

Marion must've realized she was beginning to look and sound too hysterical. She visibly took a deep breath, pushed a few stray hairs away from her forehead, and spoke a little less frantically. "I came home from doing my grocery shopping. When I put the key in the lock and opened the door, Pickles was standing right there growling at me with a glazed look in his eyes. I tried to open the door a little more so I could get in and calm him but he lunged at me. He made this awful screaming sound. I backed up and slammed the door. I could still hear him carrying on from behind the door. I gave him a few minutes to calm down and then tried to go inside again. As soon as I opened the door, he lunged at me again." Marion looked over at her neighbor as if for comfort and then continued with her story. "I decided to go around to the back door but as I opened it, Pickles was right there. He jumped at me. I shut the door and went to the garage," Marion said as she pointed in the direction of the house. Her voice was starting to quiver again. "The only other way in is through the door that connects the house to the garage. I tried to be very quiet, thinking Pickles would still be standing by the back door." The breeze was picking up and Marion absentmindedly tried to tame the stray hairs that had come loose from her ponytail. "I had barely opened the door when he threw himself at me. I managed to get him off of my sleeve," she said as she pointed to her left arm, "Then I ran over to Cara's house. By the way, this is Cara, my neighbor."

Cara smiled, looking a little embarrassed. "Hi," she said quickly.

"Hi," I replied then turned my attention back to Marion. "Has Pickles ever done anything like this before?"

"No," she shook her head, which sent the stray hairs flying in every direction. "I mean, I haven't had him very long. I officially adopted him about three weeks ago. He used to hang out by my back door, waiting for food. I'd leave a dish out there for him, and then he finally got brave enough to come in. He had already been neutered and was easy to train to a litter box. I figured he had been somebody's cat. Maybe he had gotten lost or somebody dumped him for whatever reason. I put an ad in the paper, but nobody ever called. He seemed like a pretty cool cat," Marion paused and looked back at the house with a frown. "That is, up until today."

"Has he been to the veterinarian yet?" I asked.

"No, but I was planning on taking him soon. Right now I wanted him to get used to my house."

"Are there any other pets in the house?"

Marion shook her head. "No pets, no people. It's just me and Pickles."

I instructed Marion and her neighbor to stay outside while I attempted to go inside and see Pickles. First, I went to my car and took out a blanket in case I needed protection from any possible lunging attempts made by the cat. I also brought along a cat carrier.

I informed Marion that I was going to go in through the garage entrance and that she was to shut the garage door behind me. This way, in case Pickles did make an escape attempt he'd be trapped in the garage and wouldn't get loose. My initial concern was that Pickles might be injured and I didn't want him running off. Being a former outdoor cat, Pickles may have panicked in the house at some point and possibly injured himself while trying to get out or had gotten spooked by something.

As I walked into the garage, I heard the door slam shut behind me. Marion wasn't taking any chances. She hadn't even given me time to get over to where the light switch was, so I had to fumble through the darkness until I reached the wall. Locating the switch, I turned on the light, then put my hand on the doorknob, preparing to meet Pickles. I slowly cracked open the door just an inch. Then holding the blanket with both hands, I pushed the door open a bit wider with my shoe. I looked for Pickles. The house was silent, and there was no sign of Pickles. I inched the door open a little more. I could hear Marion and her neighbor on the other side of the garage door. Marion was saying something about the fact that she'd forgotten that she'd left ice cream and frozen vegetables in the trunk of her car. I slowly opened the door an inch or two more. Still no sign of Pickles. From outside of the garage I heard the slamming of a car trunk. Marion's melted ice cream and thawed vegetables were either on their way to Cara's freezer or into the trash.

Concentrating on Pickles again, I continued to open the door enough to take a slow, quiet step inside. I peeked around the door. No Pickles. I stood still, allowing only my eyes to move. When I didn't see the cat anywhere in sight, I closed the door behind me. Taking a few baby steps, I peered down the hallway. No cat in sight. I walked to the front window and waved to Marion and Cara. I signaled for them to stay where they were. Marion was leaning on her car, chewing on her fingernails. Cara stood nearby with her arms folded across her chest and a slight smile on her face, the look of an amused skeptic. Marion and Cara made an odd pair at that moment. It was as if they were viewing two totally different scenes. In a way I guess they were.

I slowly turned back toward the room, grasping the blanket in my hands, ready to protect myself if needed. Suddenly, on the other side of the room stood a fragile looking Siamese cat. His expression seemed one of mild curiosity. I placed my blanket on the floor slowly, then knelt down on his level. Waiting only a beat, he walked over to me and sniffed my shoes. Satisfied that I didn't pose a threat, he greeted me with that unmistakable Siamese meow, turned, then trotted off out of sight. He seemed well over whatever had previously agitated him.

Before allowing Marion back into the house, I checked each room to see if I could find the possible cause of Pickles' unprovoked aggression. Everything seemed to be in order. I found the litter box in the bathroom and it appeared to be normal.

Entering the master bedroom, I found Pickles sitting on the bed. I had brought one of my interactive toys with me to use for distraction in case Pickles was agitated. I sat myself down in the middle of the room and casually began inching the toy along the carpet. Pickles watched with intense interest. He immediately crouched and sprang from the bed to pounce on the toy. As I slid the toy along the carpet, he followed with playful pounces and lightning quick leaps. Despite what emotional or physical trauma Pickles may have recently endured, at this moment he seemed like a perfectly happy cat.

After playing with him for about ten minutes, I wound the game down and Pickles stretched out next to me, rubbing his head along my leg. "I wish you could tell me what happened between you and Marion," I said to him as I reached out my hand to gently stroke the top of his head. His reply was a rumbling purr. Since he was relaxed and comfortable with me, I gave him a quick physical check to see if I could find any injuries or painful spots which could explain his sudden aggression. As far as I could tell, he had no injuries. During my brief physical examination, I noticed his skin twitched a bit when I touched him. He could still be slightly aroused from his recent ordeal with Marion, but I made a mental note of it anyway. I needed to ask Marion if she noticed his skin twitching when she petted him. Of course, the next step would be for Marion to take him to the veterinarian for a complete exam.

When I felt that enough time had elapsed for both Pickles and Marion to be reunited again, I quietly left the cat and walked to the front door. As I opened it, I noticed Marion had resorted to pacing the length of her driveway. When she heard the door open, she abruptly stopped, threw down the cigarette she was smoking, and squished it forcefully with her shoe. I imagined there were probably numerous other cigarettes squished along the length of the driveway.

"He's seems back to normal," I called to her. "You can come in now."

Marion began rapidly walking toward the house. "It's about time," she grumbled as she came up to the door. "Just what the heck is wrong with him anyway?"

"I don't know yet."

Marion looked at me with wide eyes. "You don't know yet? I thought you were the cat expert," she said, pointing her index finger just inches from my nose.

I don't like it when people call me the *cat expert*. I don't like it when owners look at me with wide eyes, expecting me to perform miracles on their cats. I really don't like it when people point their fingers at me, and at that moment, I wasn't liking Marion very much. I took a breath, stepped back a bit to get out of finger range, then offered Marion my best attempt at a friendly smile. "Why don't I help you in with your groceries, then we'll sit down and talk?"

Marion looked suspicious at first, then finally agreed. Once the groceries were put away and Cara had returned to her own home next door, Marion and I sat down at the kitchen table. Over iced tea, I had her calmly go back over the events of the day. As she talked, it was obvious she was quite hurt over the fact that the cat she had rescued had suddenly turned on her.

In gathering a history on Pickles, I asked Marion about the skin twitching I had witnessed. She said that the cat always did that whenever he was petted and in fact, he only tolerated a small amount of physical affection before moving himself out of reach.

"The first thing that needs to be done is for the veterinarian to do a complete physical exam, have Pickles tested for FELV/FIV, and get him vaccinated," I said as Marion nervously sipped her iced tea, her eyes periodically darting from side to side in search of Pickles. "Once Pickles gets a clean bill of health from the vet, we can take it from there." At that point I didn't know what had caused the sudden aggression. It could have been an isolated incident caused by the appearance of another cat outside, but as with all of my cases, a visit to the vet is the first requirement.

"I'll take him next week on my day off," Marion agreed.

"If possible, if would be better to get him there as soon as possible. Just in case this aggressive episode isn't an isolated occurrence. If there is a medical reason behind it, you'd want to know that as soon as possible."

"I'll do it as soon as I can," she said.

I suggested we go into the living room where Pickles was sitting so I could spend a little more time with him. The skin twitching concerned me. Marion reluctantly agreed to accompany me.

Pickles responded to my use of interactive toys and seemed to be normal and happy. He even went over to Marion and rubbed his head against her leg. She reached down and scratched him behind the ears. He loved it. When she stroked him along his back though, I noticed the skin twitching again. I told her to be sure and mention that to the veterinarian.

When I was sure that both cat and owner were comfortable with each other again, I left. I repeated to Marion again the importance of taking Pickles in to see the veterinarian as soon as possible. She nodded in understanding.

I called Marion the next evening to get an update on things and hopefully get news of a vet appointment but all I got was the answering machine. I left word for her to call me.

Two days went by with no return call. I left another message on her answering machine.

Another day went by.

Now there are times when I make an initial visit to a home or even when I just talk to owners on the phone when they promise to follow up at the vet and never do. I'm sure they probably feel they overreacted to the cat's misbehavior and in the calm light of day, they don't consider any other action necessary. Despite my urging, I can't force an owner to take their cat in for an examination. I had a feeling that this was the case with Marion Estee. She probably felt the crisis was over.

The following week, there was a message on my machine from Marion, apologizing for not returning my calls, but she wanted me to know that all was normal with Pickles. She had taken him to the vet for his vaccinations and he checked out fine. After listening to the message I picked up the phone and dialed Marion's number.

"Hello?"

"Marion, this is Pam Johnson Bennett. Thank you for calling me back. I'm happy that Pickles checked out okay but I just wanted to find out what the vet had to say about the skin twitching."

"Oh, I didn't mention any of that or anything about the day you came over. Pickles is normal again and I didn't want to go through all kinds of expensive tests just to be told there's nothing wrong with him. I figure if the vet didn't see anything during the exam then I had nothing to worry about."

The smile left my face, replaced with what must've been a very obvious look of concern because my dog got up from her spot across the room to sit by my side. She stared up at me with a puzzled expression. I patted her on the head to reassure her that she wasn't the cause of my worry.

Despite my urging, I couldn't convince Marion to go further with any medical checkup on Pickles. As I hung up the phone I could still hear Marion's voice ringing in my ear, emphatically telling me that she had just overreacted and was very embarrassed by the entire episode. My gut told me there was something going on with the cat that necessitated further investigation but I can't make an owner do something she doesn't want to do. I did call her vet to voice my concerns about Pickles' skin twitching. I felt it was more than just his state of agitation and wanted that written on his vet record in case the incident came up again. The veterinarian told me he would look into it the next time Pickles came in for a checkup.

Four days passed and I hadn't heard from Marion. Perhaps I was wrong about Pickles' skin twitching. It was early in the evening when I finished my last client so I used the opportunity to go to the gym for a much-needed workout. I was pounding away on the treadmill when I overheard two women talking on the stair climbers next to me. One of the women was mentioning the fact that someone's pager was going off repeatedly in one of the lockers.

"Do you think we should tell the manager so he can make an announcement?" the woman asked her friend, who was struggling to maintain some kind of a rhythm on the stair climber.

"Everyone has pagers these days. All of the women in this place will head toward the lockers."

"It must be a real emergency though. That thing was sounding off every two minutes," the first woman said as she leaned forward on the handrails of the stair climber, obviously having trouble talking and climbing at the same time.

"People with pagers are rude," the second woman sighed as she continued to attempt to find a comfortable rhythm. "They think they're so important."

Let me see, I thought to myself. A pager that was going off every two minutes. Hmmm, that sounds remarkably like the kind of pages I periodically get. And who was it who recently paged me that way? Ah yes, Marion Estee. I wonder…

I slowed my pace on the treadmill quickly until I could come to a complete stop. As I gathered up my towel and hurried past the two women on the stair climbers, I stopped long enough to thank them. "I have a funny feeling that it was my pager going off in the locker room. Thank you," I said as I rushed past them.

"Are you a doctor?" called out one of the women.

"A Feline Behaviorist," I answered without turning around.

"A *what*?" cried the woman.

"Did she say feline?" I heard one woman ask her friend. "Isn't that a…"

"CATS! She got paged about a CAT!"

I approached my locker and sure enough, I could hear my pager emitting short reminder beeps to let me know I had an unanswered page. I opened the locker, dug in my purse, and pulled out my pager. Reading the display, there were 10, yes, 10 calls from the same number. The number belonged to Marion Estee.

I fished in my purse for a quarter and called Marion from the pay phone in the locker room. She picked up on the first ring.

"I've been paging you for an hour," she said.

"I'm at the gym and my pager was in my locker," I explained.

"You don't carry it with you?"

"Marion, there are certain places and certain times where that pager isn't welcome. Now, what's the problem? Why did you page me?"

"I'm at the gas station on the corner of my street. Pickles won't let me in the house again. None of my neighbors are home. Can you come over?"

"I'll be right there," I answered, then hung up the phone, pulled my things out of the locker, and raced out of the gym. I didn't bother to shower, but I figured that Marion wouldn't be too judgmental about my hygiene.

I pulled into Marion's driveway to find her standing by her car, nervously puffing away on a cigarette. She ran to my car as soon as I came to a stop, and just as she had done before, she yanked my car door open before I'd even turned the engine off.

"This one was worse than before. He looks crazed. I think he messed all over himself too," she said in between puffs on her cigarette.

"Is the front door unlocked?" I asked.

"Yes. The keys are still hanging in the door," Marion said as she gestured toward the house, then turned back to face me. "I guess I should've listened to you, huh?" Her voice was very low, almost as if she didn't want to risk Pickles hearing this statement. "The skin twitching that you pointed out has gotten worse in the last week. He'd growl whenever I tried to pet him on the back. I assumed he was still just mad at me from that first time when I had to call you."

"Marion, Pickles needs to go to the vet for some tests."

"I realize that now, but how are we going to get him?"

"Wait here," I said as I pointed to the spot where she was standing.

I walked up to the front porch and peered in the window. Pickles was sitting in the middle of the living room. His head was hanging low. There appeared to be some pieces of feces spread across the carpet. I assumed there was probably urine in there too.

Pickles changed positions and appeared to just flop down on all fours. Whatever crisis there had been appeared to be over. He looked relaxed (or just exhausted) enough for me to enter the house.

As I opened the front door, Pickles turned and looked at me. I could see that he had in fact urinated on the carpet and from where I stood, it appeared he'd gotten a significant amount on himself as well.

I took a few steps closer. The cat stood up, and with several twitches of the skin, walked off toward the kitchen.

With Pickles out of the room, I left the house and went back to Marion who was obediently standing in the driveway.

"Give me a few minutes with him, okay?" I asked.

Marion just nodded.

From the trunk of my car I took a bottle of enzyme cleaner, used for cleaning pet stains and neutralizing odors. Then I walked back into the house.

Pickles, I assumed, was still in the kitchen, so I went into the living room and poured the enzyme cleaner onto the carpet.

After cleaning up the stains, I sat on the carpet in the living room with an interactive toy in my hands. With the long pole of the toy, I was able to reach over to the edge of the carpet so that the little target on the end of the string could slide along the floor leading into the dining room. I was hoping the sound would heighten Pickles' curiosity enough so he would come back in so I could observe him a bit.

It didn't take long for Pickles' head to appear around the corner. Catching sight of the toy, he crouched down low and inched closer. Within seconds he was doing all the normal cat moves—pouncing, pawing, and leaping. So far so good.

After several minutes of playtime, I slowed the game down, letting Pickles savor his victory. Feeling every inch the mighty hunter, he sauntered over to me and rubbed his head along the back of my hand. I petted him behind the ears and under the chin. No skin twitching so far.

At the sound of a small dog barking outside, Pickles' ears perked up and he bounded over toward the front window. With a graceful leap, he landed on the wide windowsill in order to get a better view. Everything seemed normal, but suddenly I noticed his skin twitching. I moved nearer to the window, being careful not to distract him. As I got closer, I saw that the skin twitching was getting severe as Pickles paced back and forth along the windowsill. I also noticed something else. The bottoms of the light, lacy curtains kept getting caught along his back as he paced. His lashing tail kept catching them, causing the fabric to slide along his spine. The more this happened, the more his skin twitched. Pickles began to emit loud growls and moans. Within seconds, he dropped from the windowsill, ears laid back, and started tearing around the room, crashing into furniture.

As quietly as I could, I reached behind me and pulled two sofa cushions down. I was about to put them in front of the glass stereo cabinet in order to prevent any injury to the cat, but instead, ended up having to use them for shields, as Pickles raced toward me, totally out of control. I held the pillows in front of my face as I heard the sound of teeth meeting fabric. At least it wasn't teeth meeting flesh…my flesh.

It was all over in a few minutes. I slowly lowered the pillows to locate Pickles. I spotted him sitting on the carpet a few feet away from me. His chest was heaving and he looked quite dazed. Seconds later, he was up walking around as if nothing had happened.

I walked out of the house and back to an anxious Marion to report what had happened. "Why is he doing this?" she asked.

"There could be a number of reasons. I think I have an idea though, but we need to have him checked out by the vet."

"We just did that," she said impatiently.

"This time there are some very specific things I want him checked for. We need to rule out some things, but I have a hunch about something," I answered.

"What do you think it is?"

"I'm wondering if it's Feline Hyperesthesia Syndrome."

"What the heck is that?" Marion asked while pulling a cigarette out.

"Basically, it's an excessive sensitivity to touch. The problem can present itself as unprovoked aggression. Some doctors feel the behavior is brought on by partial seizures," I answered. "The only way to get an accurate diagnosis is to first talk with your vet. We have to rule out other physiological conditions such as spinal problems, pain, skin problems, epilepsy, etc. Your vet may refer you to a specialist so an MRI can be done." I saw that Marion was getting more impatient, perhaps she was adding up the cost of all of this in her head. "First, let's get Pickles to the vet in order to discuss the options."

I went back into the house and was able to place Pickles in a carrier while Marion phoned her veterinarian's office to let them know we were on our way.

We drove in my car and I went into the examination room to be sure all of Pickles' symptoms were accurately communicated to the doctor.

The outcome of all the veterinary tests was that Pickles didn't have epilepsy, spinal problems, a skin condition, or any injury that would provoke such sudden aggression. As I expected, an appointment was made with a specialist to have an MRI done on Pickles.

The diagnosis from the specialist was Feline Hyperesthesia Syndrome. He explained to Marion that this condition was a neurotransmitter malfunction, similar to what humans refer to as panic attacks.

Feline Hyperesthesia Syndrome is not common, but any time a cat shows aggression, most especially unprovoked aggression, your veterinarian should be consulted.

Hyperesthesia more commonly appears in Siamese, Himalayan, and Abyssinian breeds. The cats affected are usually under five years of age but this condition can still show up in older cats. Cats under stress are more at risk.

Treatment Plan

In Pickles' case, after spending more time with him, I was able to determine that his stress was the result of two cats who came around his yard. Marion wasn't even aware of this because they would just come up to the window and once Pickles appeared, they'd run off. It was just luck that during a session, I witnessed an encounter.

Another form of stress for Pickles was that he wasn't allowed on the furniture and had no cat trees or perches. Being confined to ground level didn't allow him adequate feelings of safety. Cats prefer higher ground.

With the correct diagnosis, the veterinarian was able to begin Pickles on a treatment plan which involved the use of antianxiety medication.

To reduce his stress, I instructed Marion to make some environmental changes. First, we needed to find out if those two cats belonged to anyone. Marion asked the neighbors but no one knew if the cats had homes. We tried using a humane trap to catch them but they outsmarted us every time. In the meantime, we had to reduce the effect they had on Pickles. I had an idea.

First, I had Marion get rid of her curtains. They were light enough that they easily rested on Pickles' back, causing an unpleasant sensation and triggering an aggressive episode.

Next, I had to block off that window so Pickles could no longer view the cats. I also had to come up with some kind of window coverings that would please Marion but also not adversely affect Pickles. I came up with shutters. The use of shutters would allow Marion to block Pickles from the window in question, but allow him to look out other windows. Marion was pleased with the idea from a decorating standpoint and promised to get on the project right away.

Next on the list was creating some perches or cat furniture that would allow Pickles to enjoy the safety of elevated spaces. I achieved this by introducing Marion to the idea of an indoor cat tree. There are

Treatment Plan (continued)

many companies that manufacture trees that you can design yourself. You choose the carpet style, color, and height. You can also choose bark or plain wood for the supports. Some companies give you the option of rope wrapped around the tree to create a scratching post/tree combination.

Together, Marion and I were able to come up with a style that was consistent with her decor, and also satisfied the basic cat requirements.

The cat tree would be placed near a sunny window (one that Pickles enjoyed looking out of, but the other cats didn't bother with).

A very important part of Pickles' treatment plan was play therapy used in order to help relieve stress. The play sessions would also help Marion strengthen her bond with the cat.

The last part of Pickles' treatment plan concerned his diet. He would be placed on a more natural diet, free of artificial additives and preservatives. Marion had been feeding him whatever was on sale at the supermarket, supplemented with unwanted leftovers from previous meals.

Follow Up

Pickles is monitored by the veterinarian on a regular basis. His antianxiety medication has been adjusted a few times and now he's on a lower dose.

The addition of the window shutters, cat tree (and recently, a second one was added in the bedroom), nutritional program, and play therapy have all had a positive impact on Pickles. He's relaxed around company and is more receptive to physical affection—he and Marion have developed a special, loving relationship.

Strange Tastes

Many owners have seen it, heard it, and been driven nuts by it—*wool sucking*. It's the strange behavior that some cats display which consists of sucking and kneading on anything from the corner of a blanket to the hair on their owner's head. This behavior is named wool sucking because many cats focus this activity strictly on wool or wool-like fabrics, such as blankets, sweaters, and socks.

The owners of cats who occasionally suck on the corner of a sweatshirt may think it's cute, but the owners of cats who relentlessly suck and chew holes through blankets and expensive sweaters, come to me at their wit's end.

What is wool sucking and why do some cats become fixated on this bizarre oral behavior? A definitive answer is still somewhat of a mystery. A theory that behaviorists continue to explore is premature weaning. Wool sucking mimics nursing, including the *milk tread* which is the kneading motion kittens do with their paws that stimulates the release of milk from the queen. That wool sucking is caused by premature or abrupt weaning is a very valid theory to me, because many of the cats I see for wool sucking were rescued or adopted at a very early age (4–6 weeks), too early to be separated from their mother.

Just to add more confusion to an already perplexing behavior, the theory behind wool sucking has an added component. There appears to be a genetic link—particular breeds are more prone to develop this oral fixation. Oriental breeds, such as Siamese, Tonkinese, Himalayan, and Burmese tend to head the list of wool suckers. In my own files, I can narrow that down even more and say that I see predominately more Siamese cats for wool-sucking behavior than any other breed. I even had a little wool sucker myself, my mixed-breed cat Albert who, based on his head size and shape, and his dead-ringer Siamese voice, probably had Siamese blood.

I repeat, wool-sucking behavior runs the gamut, from the occasional sucker to the obsessed 24-hour-a-day destroyer of all fabrics.

Discussion among behaviorists now centers on the possibility of wool sucking being a feline version of OCD (Obsessive-Compulsive Disorder). Whether the behavior these cats display can actually be connected to the human form of OCD is still up for debate. What can be concluded from the comparison though, is that it's a compulsive-like behavior. On the mild side, many kittens with this fixation seem to outgrow it as their attention is diverted to more interesting activities. I was able to help Albert overcome his fondness for my earlobe by having a toy with me and diverting his attention to playtime. He was 11 weeks old at the time this behavior presented itself and within three weeks his need to suck on my earlobe had been forgotten. My sore earlobe breathed a sigh of relief. When I look back, I realize how lucky I was compared to what some of my clients have been through.

Wishbone was a cat referred to me by a local veterinarian because of her overpowering appetite for her owner's clothes. The cat had a complete exam and work-up and was determined to be in perfect health—well, physically anyway.

When I knocked on Vanessa Teague's apartment door, I was met by a young woman holding a pair of socks out in front of her. The red socks sported numerous holes in them, some still moist, indicating a very recent crime.

"My roommate forgot our rule about not leaving clothes out. She left these on top of the dryer this morning." She transferred both socks to one hand and shook them in the direction of the mixed-breed cat that had sauntered up to the door. "You're a bad cat, *bad cat!*" she scolded, then turned her attention back toward me. "You see what we're up against? I just don't understand why she's doing this." She motioned for me to come in. "I'm sorry, I'm just so frustrated." She held out her hand, the one without the sock. "I'm Vanessa and that's Libby, my roommate, over there." She gestured toward the young woman sitting on the sofa. I couldn't help but notice the outfit: red shirt, red and black checked pants and...bare feet. I assumed the socks she had planned to wear this morning were now crumpled in Vanessa's grip.

My first question to Vanessa concerned Wishbone's age and background. She answered that she was 1 ½ years old and a mixed breed. Vanessa had picked her up in the parking lot at her office when she was just a kitten. The vet had estimated her age to be about five weeks at the time. She was quite thin and needed lots of care. "It was touch and go for a while, but Libby and I saw her through it," Vanessa said.

My next question concerned how long ago the behavior had started. Vanessa let out an audible sigh before answering. "She nursed on shoelaces when she was a kitten, but we didn't think anything of it because she never chewed them or caused any damage. We just figured that with her rough start in life she needed a little extra comfort."

"When did it become more serious?" I asked, while watching Wishbone, who appeared to be sizing up the jacket I'd laid across my briefcase. Just to be on the safe side, I picked it up and put it on my lap. Wishbone looked disappointed.

"About six months ago we began to notice wet spots on the blankets and on any clothes we left out. At first I thought she was peeing on them but they didn't have any smell," Vanessa said.

At that point, Libby entered the conversation, pulling her legs up onto the sofa and sitting cross-legged, with her bare feet tucked underneath. "We started seeing these tufts and knots on the blankets and a few sweaters. Then we caught her in the act," Libby shook her head. "Vanessa has tried everything. We've scolded her, squirted her with water, we even tried giving her a sock of her own but she still chewed on our stuff."

Vanessa looked over at Wishbone with a sad expression. "We thought that if we always kept our clothes put away, she'd eventually forget about them."

"Putting my clothes away isn't always easy to remember because I work nights and I get home late," Libby added. "I'm too tired to hang everything up."

"Follow me," instructed Vanessa as she stood up and motioned to me. I was led into a bedroom where there was a chair blocking the door to the closet. "We had to put this in front of the door because if the closet isn't latched just right, Wishbone can open it."

As Vanessa moved the chair aside, true to form, Wishbone was right there, ready for the opportunity to have a little wool snack. Libby reached down and scooped Wishbone up so Vanessa could open the closet door. As I looked inside I noticed the rod was exceptionally high. Obviously, a measure they had to resort to in order to keep Wishbone from reaching up and nibbling at the bottoms of the clothes. Vanessa then closed the door and put the chair back in its guard position so Libby could release the struggling cat. Wishbone then immediately hopped up on the chair and stared at the door as if willing it to open.

"I'm about at the end of my rope," confessed Vanessa. "Wishbone is really my responsibility so I've paid Libby for the clothes that she's ruined, besides having to replace my own things. I work part-time because I'm still in college, so I can't afford to keep doing this."

Libby saw that Vanessa was beginning to get choked up so she took over. "Vanessa thought she might have to put Wishbone to sleep. She couldn't give her away, knowing the damage she'd cause. When we told this to the vet, she suggested we call you. Do you think you can help?"

Both Vanessa and Libby looked me right in the eyes, hoping I'd say the word they needed to hear. I even held Wishbone's attention at that point. I can never in good conscience just blindly say "yes." I have to qualify it with "I'll do my best." Granted, it wasn't the answer they were hoping for, but I did feel optimistic about the situation. I'd had enough success with wool-sucking cats to feel we stood a good chance at conquering Wishbone's obsession.

Treatment Plan

The first instruction I gave Libby and Vanessa was to continue what they'd already been doing—keeping all laundry put away. In Libby's case, if it meant keeping a hamper in her room so she could just toss her clothes in there, then that's what she'd have to do. They both needed to be faultless in their efforts to keep the wool out of Wishbone's mouth. It wouldn't always have to be this strict, but for now we needed to remove all temptation.

Step two involved an immediate cease of all punishment. Since this was a compulsive behavior truly out of Wishbone's control that may or may not be triggered by stress, I didn't want them to add fuel to the fire.

Step three involved an interesting approach to a wool-sucking treatment: dietary manipulation. I asked Vanessa what she fed Wishbone. Her answer was that the cat ate a high-quality canned food that the vet had recommended. Apparently, Wishbone had always been a finicky eater and had trouble gaining weight. As a kitten, canned food was the only kind she'd accept, so they'd been feeding her a small can in the morning and one at night.

"I'd like you to add dry food to her diet," I said, explaining that there has been much success in treating wool-sucking cats by increasing the fiber in their diet. Since at this point in her life Wishbone was not underweight, I wanted Vanessa to use a prescription, high-fiber dry food available from her vet. "Leave a bowl out for her to eat freely. It may be enough to satisfy her craving. Begin to wean her off of the canned food by feeding her smaller amounts, eventually phasing it out totally."

"How much dry food should we leave out?" asked Vanessa.

"A big bowl, so that when Wishbone gets a craving she always has that as an alternative to the fabric. The food is used for weight reduction so it's lower in fat and calories than what you're feeding her now."

Of course, I also gave my usual instructions for regularly scheduled play therapy, and how to use it for diversion should Wishbone remain

Treatment Plan (continued)

fixated on the closet door. It would also help in cases in which wool sucking was intensified by stress.

Finally, I told Vanessa and Libby that if they didn't see enough of an improvement through the use of behavior modification and dietary manipulation, I would talk to their vet about the use of drug therapy. Even though there is no proven connection between wool-sucking behavior in cats and OCD in humans, antianxiety drugs used for compulsive disorders, such as Prozac, have been effective. Prozac and Prozac-like drugs have been used to treat tail sucking, tail chasing, excessive grooming, wool sucking and other OCD-like behavior disorders. I don't view Prozac as a wonder drug and I certainly don't ever rush to recommend it to a client. I always try behavior modification first and, in this case, wanted to make sure Vanessa and Libby knew that I was counting on them to work diligently during the next few weeks.

Vanessa and Libby both agreed to do everything they could when it came to using the behavior modification techniques. After giving me a big hug and saying how she'd do anything to keep Wishbone, Vanessa led me to the front door. I told her that I expected an update in no more than one week, unless she needed to speak to me sooner.

Having said goodbye, I left, and heard Libby say to Vanessa as the door closed behind me, "Do you believe they give *Prozac* to *cats* now?"

Follow Up

After one week, Vanessa called with an update. Wishbone's wool sucking had decreased by almost 90 percent. There had been one incident with the sleeve of a sweatshirt that was left dangling out of the hamper. Libby had come home extremely tired from work and didn't quite get all of the shirt into the hamper. Vanessa said that there was only one tiny hole in it though, not the four or five that Wishbone usually inflicted on sleeves.

At the end of the second week, I hadn't heard from Vanessa. I assumed that all was going well. Four days later I received a call that Wishbone had chewed on Libby's socks while she was wearing them. She'd been asleep on the sofa and Wishbone seized the opportunity. I was very disappointed.

"How much of the dry food is she eating?" I asked. "How did she adjust to the dry food?"

There was a moment of silence before Vanessa answered. "We still give her the canned food. She kept looking for it in the morning so we thought we'd feed her both dry and canned."

"She needs to be weaned off of the canned food so we can provide an adequate amount of dietary fiber."

"Okay," Vanessa agreed.

The next update I received was the following week. Wishbone was happily eating her high-fiber dry food exclusively. My instruction to Vanessa was to keep all clothing out of Wishbone's reach for one more week and then I wanted her to heave a decoy sock on the floor as an experiment. We needed to see where we stood in terms of Wishbone's wool-sucking desire.

"Well, we've got plenty of socks without mates thanks to Wishbone, so we'll be able to do it," Vanessa joked.

The report one week later was great. Wishbone ignored the sock completely and continued to stick to her dry food.

One year later, Wishbone has continued to be a reformed wool sucker and Libby has happily gone back to her habit of tossing her clothes on the floor. Vanessa told me that she wished the behavior modification for the cat would've had a more lasting effect on Libby's lack of neatness.

Do Cats Cry?

Willy was the king of the house. At 16 years of age, this Border Collie mix had life figured out. He slept late into the morning, and
then after enjoying a leisurely breakfast of his favorite prescription
senior food, he'd stroll outside to catch a few rays. His owners,
Wanda and Arnie Tansmore and their young daughter, Angela, all
doted on him. To Angela, Willy was her big brother, often keeping
her out of trouble by barking whenever she ventured too close to
the property's edge.

Another member of the family who cherished Willy was Eek, the
approximately 12-year old orange tabby who shared the Tansmore
home with him. Eek had been adopted by the Tansmores after
Arnie and Willy found her 10 years ago in a ditch by the side of the
road one evening during Arnie and Willy's ritual late-night walks.
She'd apparently been hit by a car and had managed to crawl to the
ditch by the side of the road, where she collapsed. Willy was the
one who noticed her and barked, tugging repeatedly at his leash. At
first, Arnie didn't see anything and tried to coax Willy away from
the spot for fear the dog's loud barking would disturb the neighbors,
but Willy stood his ground. Remembering that his dog only barked
when there was something to bark about, Arnie walked over to the
ditch and bent down for a closer look. "It better not be a skunk
you're leading me to," he half-jokingly told the dog.

It was difficult to see, but Arnie thought he saw something orange
mixed in with all the mud. "There go my new shoes," he said as he
made his way into the ditch and saw a cat crumpled in a heap, covered with mud and blood.

"Oh, God," he said as he tied Willy's leash to his belt so he'd have
both hands free. "I think it's dead," he cried as he touched the life-
less animal. When there was no response, Arnie gently picked up
the cat and carried it out of the ditch. Willy stood silently watching, not taking his eyes off the creature for a second.

Arnie laid the cat on the road then removed his shirt. "Can't bring it back like that for Wanda to see," he said as he spread the shirt out and placed the cat inside. As he began wrapping the cat up, he suddenly felt a slight movement. Stunned, he got down on his hands and knees and put his hand on the cat's chest. "It's breathing, Willy," he said and carefully and quickly wrapped the cat up. "We've got to get it to the doctor."

Home they ran, a shirtless Arnie with the cat in his arms, followed by Willy who was still tethered to Arnie's belt.

Wanda saw her bare-chested husband running up the driveway with the dog pulling him awkwardly from side to side. She came running out in her robe to see what had happened.

"Wanda, go get me the car keys," he shouted as she came rushing toward him. "We found an injured cat. I've got to get it to the emergency clinic." Without hesitation, Wanda spun around and raced back in the house. She and Arnie had spent many nights nursing injured birds and rabbits back to health, so there was no question about coming to the aid of a cat.

Running out with the keys, Wanda asked if the cat was badly injured. Arnie nodded his head and told her not to look. She smiled at her husband and said, "I love you," as she opened the car door for him. "Can you do this alone?" she asked as he placed the cat in the passenger side of the front seat.

"Yeah, just take Willy," he said, straightening back up and untying the dog's leash from his belt. "Good boy," Arnie said to Willy and gave him a pat on the head. "You found the cat, good boy."

Wanda and Willy stood in the driveway and watched as the car pulled onto the road and out of sight.

With a grim prognosis, Arnie returned home to inform his wife that the cat had been severely injured by a car. At first Arnie thought the kindest thing to do would be to have her put to sleep, but while the doctor was examining the cat, she opened her eyes and looked at Arnie. He told Wanda that the cat didn't take her eyes off him until they carried her out of the room. "I couldn't let her down," he said sadly.

"*Her*?" asked Wanda. "It's a female?" She'd always wanted a female cat.

"Yeah," he answered. "And I bet she's a knockout when she's not covered in mud."

And that was it. From that moment on, Arnie and Wanda checked on the cat's progress every day. She had been transferred to their regular vet, who was much closer, so they were able to visit her often.

Wanda ran ads in the newspaper and put up posters, hoping someone would claim the cat, but there was no response.

Eleven days later, the cat was well enough to be discharged from the hospital and begin her long road back to recovery. With two broken legs, several lacerations and a wired jaw, it would take much nursing on the part of Wanda and Arnie to get her back in good health. They had already made a financial commitment for the cat's medical expenses, and now they realized that the strong emotional commitment was there as well.

As soon as their two-year old Angela caught sight of the double-splinted cat, she shrieked "*eek!*" From that point on, she continued to shout "eek!" whenever she saw her. The orange cat officially came to be known as *Eek*.

From the moment Eek was brought home, Willy stayed by her side. Eek slept in the warmth of Willy's soft fur and was groomed by his big sloppy tongue. During the day, Willy left Eek's side only long enough to eat and go outside for the necessary dog duties.

In time, as Eek healed and the splints and wire were removed, Willy instituted his own form of physical therapy by gently pushing Eek with his nose to get her to chase him. It didn't take much coaxing because without the splints, Eek was a streak of lightning. Together, they zoomed around the house, sliding around corners, and skidding to sudden stops at the front door.

For the next 10 years, Eek and Willy were almost of one mind. They patrolled the yard together, ate together (often sampling each other's food), and slept in the same position they had slept in from day one, with Eek nestled in Willy's fur.

Now as time and age crept up on them, Eek and Willy spent most of their time lounging in the sun and taking slow strolls around the property. Since finding Eek 10 years ago, Willy had been protective of Eek, and would bark at any dog or cat that attempted to wander onto the property. Eek didn't have a care in the world because she had Willy.

It was the winter that Nashville experienced several ice storms. Icy road conditions would occur suddenly due to the abruptly falling temperatures. Rain would turn to sleet and make driving a nightmare. It was during one of these sudden weather changes that Arnie and Willy found themselves in trouble.

The afternoon started out with a steady rain. Willy had been at the vet for an examination to keep tabs on a developing heart condition. Arnie had dropped him off that morning and was to pick him up at 4:30. Eek had been very restless that day without her buddy. Distracted, she paced and paced, stopping only to look out the window or check for signs of Willy's return.

When Arnie drove to the vet, the conditions were beginning to get slippery, but he was a careful driver and was used to Nashville's icy roads.

At the vet, there was a 20-minute wait before Arnie could speak with the doctor due to an incoming emergency. Once Arnie was called into the exam room, Willy was immediately brought to him. They greeted each other enthusiastically and moments later the vet entered. Willy's heart condition had deteriorated slightly so Arnie was given a new prescription for the dog. A follow-up appointment was made and Arnie left with Willy.

Even though Arnie was a careful driver, he was unable to control the actions of another, less careful driver who lost control of his car and crashed into the passenger side of the car. Arnie's injuries were not too serious, just cuts and bruises, but he was badly shaken up. When he regained his composure, he immediately looked over at his dog who lay motionless. Arnie called out his name, but he knew there'd be no response. The right side of the car was completely crumpled. Willy hadn't survived the accident.

The next week was filled with grief, confusion, and pain. Arnie, still shaken from the accident, was recovering from physical injuries, but like the rest of his family, had a long way to go in terms of his emotional pain.

The absence of Willy was unbearable for everyone. Even the neighbors had trouble looking out of their windows for the familiar Border Collie on the front lawn and not seeing him.

While Arnie, Wanda, and their daughter tried to comfort each other, Eek quietly went about searching for Willy, keeping watch at the window, taking very little time to eat, and pacing the house at night after everyone went to bed, before finally settling down. Because she was keeping to herself and exhibiting much of her restlessness only after the family had retired for the night, the Tansmores mistakenly thought she was doing surprisingly well.

One afternoon, two weeks later, there was a sudden commotion in the driveway. A high-pitched yapping sound was heard from the squirming, wiggling, tiny bundle Arnie carried in his arms. Angela came running out of the house with Wanda behind her. As soon as Angela saw the Golden Retriever puppy she squealed with delight and insisted on holding him.

Arnie watched his giggling daughter. He hadn't even seen her smile in two weeks. He and Wanda had discussed the situation and decided to get a new puppy to alleviate the pain caused by Willy's death.

Eek watched the sudden burst of activity from the window. When she saw Angela carrying the puppy up the steps and into the house, she took off to the safety of the bedroom. Arnie and Wanda's attempts to help Eek become friends with the new puppy were met with hisses, swats, and long episodes of hiding. Life for Eek started to consist of being chased, pushed, knocked down, and relentlessly bothered by the exuberant puppy. Four months later, things went from bad to worse. Eek ran away. She didn't go far, but it was enough to put a scare into everybody. She was found three days later by a neighbor a few houses down. Eek had sought refuge in the neighbor's rusted-out tool shed. She had been squeezing in and out of the hole in the back of the shed.

Upon Eek's return, I was called. The Tansmores didn't know what to do to help Eek accept Bob, the puppy.

During my housecall to the Tansmores, I noticed all of the family pictures on the walls and on the tables. Willy and Eek were front and center in almost every one. There were beautiful pictures of Willy and Eek sleeping together and playing in the yard. The bond they shared was evident in every snapshot.

As I interviewed Wanda and Arnie, Bob bounced around the room with his tail wagging in excitement. He impatiently jumped from Wanda to Arnie to me in search of attention. Arnie's attempts at reprimanding the puppy were met with total disregard on Bob's part. The puppy had selective hearing.

When I went into the room where Eek was hiding, I was immediately struck by her appearance. Even taking her age into consideration, the cat I was looking at bore little resemblance to the cat in the photographs. This cat was thin with dull, dry fur. Her eyes appeared vacant. She sat like a statue on top of the tall dresser in the bedroom. It was her usual spot, Wanda had told me when we entered the room. No wonder, I thought to myself, it's the one spot where the dog can't get to her.

While the Tansmores had thought they were doing the best thing for their family by attempting to have the puppy ease their grief, they created a worse situation for poor little Eek. She didn't get to grieve for Willy and was unable to find comfort through her family.

There's a balance that needs to be struck between the cat as a *cat* and the cat as a *family member*. I'm always preaching to owners to remember that although they view their cat as their child, they need to make sure to fulfill the cat's *cat needs*. As I described in the beginning of this book, it involves looking at your world through your cat's eyes and providing for her emotional, physical, and mental health. You must also balance that with an understanding that cats experience many of the same emotions that we do. For example: stress, depression, fear, etc. And, let's not forget *grief*. Imagine Eek's overwhelming confusion when Willy disappeared from her life. Here is a cat, a creature of habit, who had everything in her life turned upside down. She can still pick up Willy's scent, but he's nowhere to be found. To make matters worse, Eek looks at her family, Wanda, Arnie and Angela, and sees them all acting differently. Like I said, *everything* in her life had been turned upside down. She became anxious and stressed.

For a stressed cat still grieving for her lost companion, the sudden addition of a puppy was certainly unwelcome and ill-timed. Eek lost every area of security because the puppy would just bulldoze right over her. Life became a day-to-day search for a safe place to hide.

Training a new puppy is a lot of work, so the Tansmores became very occupied with that overwhelming task. Without realizing it, Eek was being lost in the shuffle.

"But we got Bob partially for Eek too. We thought she'd want another companion," said Arnie, defending himself.

"Eek needed recovery time and she needed your attention to let her know that everything in her life had not changed. And don't forget that she's an older cat. The addition of an energetic puppy can be too much," I answered.

"Do cats cry, I wonder?" asked Wanda.

"Cats are very stoic but they feel many of the same emotions that we do," I responded. "Because they appear so self-reliant, we sometimes overlook the pain they may be feeling."

"Eek needed us and we let her down," Arnie said, shaking his head.

"Eek needs you *now* and you can be there for her," I said as I watched the puppy begin to chew on the corner of my briefcase. "Let's start right now with Bob."

Treatment Plan

The first order of business involved the Tansmores making two important appointments. The first one was with the vet in order to check Eek's current physical health. I didn't like the way she looked and wanted to make sure there wasn't an underlying medical condition.

The second appointment would be with a dog trainer that I knew and worked with often. Aside from trying to get Eek and Bob together, the dog needed some serious obedience training. Bob was a bundle of misdirected, uncontrolled, puppy energy. Without proper training he'd be the kind of pet no one likes—the kind that jumps all over guests, pulls on his leash, ignores his owner's commands, and is the terror of the neighborhood. If you want to make your neighbors hate you, get a big dog who can't be controlled.

I explained how with proper training, Wanda and Arnie could use a leash and voice commands to teach Bob to respect Eek's personal space. The cat needed to feel safe in her own home. Up until this point, she had never had the chance to decide whether she could like Bob or not. From the moment he entered the house, she had to go on full security alert. Even without considering the fact that she was still grieving for Willy, the puppy was too intrusive for Eek.

Treatment Plan (continued)

In training, one of the most important commands for Bob to learn in terms of getting Eek's approval would be "down stay." Having Bob in a relaxed, low-to-the-ground position, and being able to keep him there would facilitate acceptance on Eek's behalf as she began venturing out into the main part of the house again.

Eek also needed exclusive time with her owners. I instructed Wanda and Arnie to make time each day for her. That time could include play, petting, grooming, whatever Eek enjoyed. Angela was to do the same for Eek as well.

Eek loved being outdoors and the Tansmores had stopped letting her out since she had run away, for fear that she would disappear again. I understood their concern but felt Eek was depressed over her imprisonment. I recommended that they get a leash and harness for her so she could once again enjoy the outdoors. Wanda said that Eek really just loved to lay on the front porch and sun herself. With the leash, Wanda said, she could go out with her and take her much-needed daily tea break.

I instructed Wanda and Arnie on how to conduct low-key play-therapy sessions for Eek. I wasn't sure how energetic she'd be during play but I thought it best for the Tansmores to start gradually and let Eek determine the pace. It didn't have to be a lightning-quick game for Eek to benefit. Having her predatory instincts awakened and dusted off might add a little spark to her life.

Follow Up

Bob went through obedience training and is an almost perfectly behaved dog. He responds to verbal commands and is excellent at "down stay" except when outside. The distraction of other dogs still causes him to have momentary lapses in judgment, but Arnie and Wanda continue to work with him.

Eek learned to accept Bob in her life. While the bond wasn't the same as the one that she had shared with Willy, she did begin sleeping with him. Instead of curling up at his chest the way she did with Willy, she chose to snooze on top of Bob. Thrilled that she viewed him as a comfortable bed, Bob didn't even mind when her long tail tickled his ears.

Eek's initial physical exam was unremarkable except the vet did recommend that she be given vitamins since she had lost weight. With the help of behavior modification and the healing power of time, she continued to improve emotionally.

Three years after Willy's death, Eek was diagnosed with a cancerous tumor. Despite the best medical care, her prognosis was very grave. Wanda and Arnie agonized over what to do. Finally, as they watched their precious cat become weaker, they made the painful decision to end her suffering. Wanda called the vet and made an appointment for the next morning.

Eek never made it to the vet, she quietly died in Wanda's arms that evening, surrounded by the family that loved her so. The next day, Arnie dug a grave and she was buried alongside her beloved Willy so he could once again watch over her.

Wanda and Arnie were very careful in dealing with Bob's grief over Eek. They made sure he received plenty of love and attention. Wanda called me and asked about getting another puppy or kitten. "How will I know when the time is right to get another pet?" she asked.

Follow-Up *(continued)*

"You'll just *know*," was my answer.

Seven months later, a dirty, flea-infested, emaciated, white kitten showed up in their backyard and never left. Today, *Kelsey* is a healthy, beautiful full-grown cat who lavishes much attention on Bob.

"I guess it was the right time," Wanda told me over the phone one day.

Yep.

Additional Note

When dealing with the loss of a pet, remember that surviving pets need to go through their own grieving process. The extra time you spend playing with them and petting them can help make it a less traumatic and lonely transition period.

I've found that it isn't so much the *holding* and *clutching* of the pet that's as vital as just spending time engaging in play activity and petting. Sometimes when we're grieving, we hold onto the surviving cat too tightly, almost clinging to her. This can send a red flag to the cat that something *really, really* bad is happening in the house. It might even make the cat more nervous. Be comforting, but not suffocating. Strike a balance so that both you and your cat find comfort in each other.

Focusing more attention on your cat may actually have the added bonus of helping you through your own grief. When I lost my father a few years ago, I noticed that whenever I found myself sobbing and feeling truly hopelessly lost, my cats would come around meowing. They paced restlessly around me and meowed louder and louder. I realized that they'd never witnessed that behavior from me before. I must've been confusing them and making them anxious. To ease their discomfort I would get an interactive toy out and do a play-therapy session. Before I knew it, I was feeling better, and enjoying watching my cats comically stalking and chasing the toy. At the end of the game I'd wonder which one of us was actually doing the comforting and which one was being comforted. That's what I love about cats—they teach me so much about life.

Before ending this section on the more unusual behaviors, I thought I'd include a story about an *owner's* out-of-the-ordinary behavior. And, since this book has focused on undesirable and frustrating feline behaviors, I wanted to end with the story that truly reflects the unconditional love that can happen between a cat and an owner, especially when they least expect it. This love enables us to find solutions to our cats' seemingly mystifying behaviors and enables our cats to endure our often clumsy attempts at communication

A Lesson in Love

Mr. Vinsley was one of the most memorable clients I've ever known. Originally from England, he was an older man who had been a widower for many years and lived in a beautiful mansion in Kentucky.

"My problem is very unusual," he said at the beginning of our phone call, but he refused to go into any greater detail.

"Please, Mr. Vinsley," I urged him, "I prefer to have an idea of what behavior a cat is displaying in case I feel a visit to the vet is needed."

"I promise you, a vet is not required for this situation," he replied. Pausing a moment, he added, "I assure you, I'm not a crackpot."

I began to discuss my fee with him, but he interrupted again. "It doesn't matter—I'll pay whatever you charge."

I explained to him that if I got to his house and felt a vet visit was required, I'd have to reschedule our session. He agreed.

Four days later I was headed to Kentucky.

The Vinsley residence was located on a beautiful and secluded road. The long driveway led up to a magnificent house. There were two cars parked in the driveway—a shining black Mercedes and a dusty gray Honda. I parked next to the Honda.

I was greeted at the door by the housekeeper. She eyed my armful of cat toys and raised an eyebrow.

"I'm the feline behavior consultant," I smiled.

"The cat *shrink*," she corrected me.

I was led into the living room, where I was told Mr. Vinsley would join me shortly. I sat down on the huge couch and glanced around the antique-filled room. Massive pieces of furniture dominated the long walls. Each vase and statue looked as if it held a fascinating history. Heavy draperies hung from the large windows, blocking the sun. It felt like being in a museum.

While I waited for Mr. Vinsley to appear, I neatly arranged all my cat toys on the carpet next to the couch. My notebook was opened and my pen sat ready to take down client history. All I needed was my client. So I waited. And waited. My client was now twelve minutes late.

The housekeeper reappeared in the doorway. "Mr. Vinsley apologizes for the delay. He'll be with you directly," she said coolly. "Would you care for something to drink?"

"No, thank you," I replied, and the housekeeper disappeared quickly.

Another ten minutes went by. I found myself starting to get sleepy. The sofa was quite comfortable and the room rather dark. "I'll give him five more minutes and then I'm leaving," I said to myself, or at least I *thought* I'd said it to myself.

"Forgive me, Miss Johnson."

I jerked my head up and looked in the direction of the voice with the British accent. In the doorway stood a very distinguished, thin man in a three-piece suit. I guessed his age to be late seventies. He had a full head of silver hair, combed very stylishly. He stepped toward me, offering his hand. "Please forgive my rudeness," he said as we greeted each other. "I had to take a very important but rather annoying phone call."

"I understand," I nodded. "Now, why don't we get started?"

I began to reach for my notebook, but he stood up and started for the door.

"Let's have some tea," he said. "Or would you prefer coffee?"

I started to say that I had already declined his housekeeper's offer, but he wouldn't take no for an answer. So tea it was.

As we drank our tea and ate cookies baked by the housekeeper (who shot me another skeptical look when she brought in the tray), I began to question Mr. Vinsley about his cat. "What behavior has your cat been displaying?" I asked, preparing to take notes.

"Oh, he's a fine cat," he stated as he took a bit of cookie. "There's nothing wrong with his behavior."

I looked up from my notebook. "There's *nothing* wrong with his behavior?"

He saw my reaction and leaned back in his chair. "I do have a problem with my cat, but it doesn't have anything to do with his behavior."

"All right, then. How can I help you?" I was tempted to remind him that I was, after all, a feline *behavior* consultant, but there was something about this man I liked. He seemed sincere. Sincere about what, I didn't know, but sincere nonetheless.

"I need you to find a good home for my cat."

I took off my glasses and rubbed my eyes. "Mr. Vinsley, I don't handle animal adoptions. I deal with animal behavior. I can give you the names of some wonderful people I know who…"

"No," he interrupted. "I specifically want *you* to find him a home."

"Why me?"

"Miss Johnson, I've read your books, seen you on TV, and heard about the work you do. You really understand cats. My cat, Dancer, is all I have, and I want the very best for him. I'll pay you for all the time you spend searching."

I was confused. "Why do you need to find him another home?"

Mr. Vinsley looked at me. I saw his eyes get misty for just a moment, and then he regained his composure. "Mr. Vinsley, are you all right?" I asked.

"I have cancer," he said in almost a whisper. He then went on to explain his reason for calling me. His doctor had told him he had less than nine months to live. He was not afraid to die, he assured me. After all, he had lived a good 77 years. He had every comfort, had never wanted for anything, and was willing to face the end of his life with dignity. All of his business was in order. He had no family and wanted the money from his estate to go to cancer research, children's charities, and several animal-welfare organizations.

"There's just one important thing left to do," Mr. Vinsley said sadly. "I need to take care of Dancer. I found him four years ago and we've been best friends ever since. I need you to find him a home while I'm still alive. I want to know for sure that he'll be getting the love and care he deserves. I'll provide for his medical and food expenses." He looked down at his hands and then at me. "I know anyone else would think I'm a foolish old man, worrying about some cat, but he's been by my side through these very tough last years. When I was too sick to get out of bed, Dancer stayed right with me. He's a wonderful friend, and I want to make sure he lives a good life without me."

I didn't know what to say. Mr. Vinsley stood up, breaking my awkward silence.

"I'll introduce you to Dancer." With that, he left the room.

It was then that I realized I'd been holding my breath as he'd been talking. I hadn't been expecting anything like this.

A few minutes later Mr. Vinsley came back, holding a gray cat in his arms. Dancer was a tough-looking male cat who had obviously seen more than his share of fights before becoming a resident at the Vinsley home. He was a huge cat, not fat, but large. Both ears were torn at the tips and his nose bore several old scars.

Despite his rough exterior, Dancer's personality was sweet and gentle. Wrapped in his owner's arms, his loud purr sounded like an old car engine. Mr. Vinsley placed him on the floor, and he walked right over to greet me. Not content with just being petted, Dancer jumped into my lap and nuzzled me with his face.

Mr. Vinsley had found Dancer sitting on his car one cold winter morning. Having no fondness for cats at all, he promptly chased Dancer off the car, and that was that! Or so Mr. Vinsley thought. Every morning for the next week, there was this gray cat sitting on the roof of his beautiful Mercedes.

One morning as Mr. Vinsley watched the news on TV from his bed, he heard that the temperature would continue to drop during the day. It would be frigid by evening. Even though he didn't like cats, he hated the thought that the poor creature might freeze outside. Surely he must belong to someone. Mr. Vinsley planned on telling the owner of the cat to keep him on his own property! Perhaps he has a collar, Mr. Vinsley thought. So he quickly dressed and went out, fully expecting to find the big gray cat lounging on his car as usual. He opened the front door, felt the blast of cold air, and looked out. No cat.

Mr. Vinsley had never liked animals, and yet he found himself checking outside every few minutes, waiting for the cat. He kept telling himself that all he wanted to do was to find the owner of this pesky feline.

When the housekeeper arrived home from her morning shopping, she found Mr. Vinsley in the kitchen in his robe, spooning a can of tuna into a dish. She didn't ask him what he was doing. He hadn't been eating well lately, so if he wanted to eat tuna at seven in the morning, why bother him?

Mr. Vinsley hurried outside and placed the dish of tuna on the roof of his car, then went back to his warm house to wait. His plan was to take the cat to the local shelter if it had no identification. He'd get rid of that stray one way or the other.

A widower for 25 years, Mr. Vinsley had outlived his only son. With no grandchildren and no surviving relatives, he was very used to a life of solitude. He spent his days reading, listening to music, and walking around the beautiful grounds surrounding his house. He was comfortable being alone and was not at all interested in making friends or engaging in silly chatter with neighbors. His housekeeper jokingly referred to him as "Scrooge."

By the end of the day, the tuna, now quite frozen, was removed from the car. The housekeeper watched but knew better than to say anything.

"Have it your way, you stupid cat," Mr. Vinsley said as he went back inside the house and dumped the can in the garbage. Just before going to bed that night, he stuck his head out the front door one more time to check for the annoying cat. He wasn't out there, so Mr. Vinsley locked the door and went to bed.

At about 2:00 A.M., Mr. Vinsley woke up. He swears it was a terrible thirst that drove him out of bed and down the stairs to the kitchen. Along the way, he stopped for a quick peek out the front door—still no cat sitting on the car. But just as Mr. Vinsley was about to close the door he caught sight of something limping toward him. Hobbling up the driveway was the gray cat. His fur was matted and dirty, and his right front paw dangled helplessly in the air. Mr. Vinsley stepped out onto the porch, but as soon as he did, the gray cat stopped.

"I'm not going to hurt you," he said to the cat. "Come here and I'll help you."

The cat just looked at him, not moving. Mr. Vinsley didn't know if he should go in to get more food. What if the cat ran off? But he knew he had to do something soon—the cold air was going right through his thin robe.

Leaving the front door open, he slowly stepped backward into the house and padded into the kitchen, where he dumped some leftover chicken onto a large plate. He was afraid the cat would be gone, but when he got back to the front porch, there the cat was, standing in the driveway with his paw in the air.

Mr. Vinsley placed the food on the porch and leaned against the doorway. The old man and the cat just looked at each other.

Mr. Vinsley really hadn't cared about anybody in a long time, and he didn't know why he was so concerned about this cat now. There was just something about him. Here were two tough old guys, so used to being alone that they didn't even know how to ask for help.

"I generally don't care for your kind, you know," Mr. Vinsley said to the hesitant feline, "but please let me help you. Come on, it's too cold for me to be out here."

A few minutes passed. Mr. Vinsley was shivering. The cat was watching him intently; he seemed to be making a decision. Warily, the old gray cat limped up to the porch, sniffed at the plate of food, then weakly hobbled past it and through the open doorway.

Amazed that the cat had voluntarily walked into the house, Mr. Vinsley followed him in and closed the door. "I don't blame you for passing up the chicken," he said to the cat. "Regina's not a very good cook."

After some hesitation, the cat allowed Mr. Vinsley to examine his injured paw. It would need medical attention first thing in the morning. In the meantime, the scruffy old thing would spend the night in the kitchen. As Mr. Vinsley bent down to scoop him up, the cat darted off on his three good legs in the direction of the stairs. Before he could be stopped, he clumsily hobbled up toward the bedrooms.

Planing to retrieve the nuisance cat in a moment, Mr. Vinsley went back to lock the front door. Cold and tired, he then climbed the stairs. Figuring that the frightened cat would be hiding under one of the beds, he switched on the light to begin his search. But the cat had already decided that being *on* Mr. Vinsley's bed was much more comfortable. There he was, curled up at the foot of the huge bed.

"You could've at least chosen one of the guest rooms," Mr. Vinsley commented. But he was too tired to argue, so he crawled under the covers, stretched his feet out next to the cat, and turned out the light. "Don't get too used to this. You're leaving in the morning."

The following morning, on the way to his own doctor's appointment, Mr. Vinsley dropped the cat off at the nearest veterinary hospital.

It was at this visit to the doctor that Mr. Vinsley learned he had cancer. Depressed and frightened, he drove home, almost forgetting to stop at the vet's. In fact, when he realized he was about to pass the animal hospital, he seriously considered just leaving the cat there for the vet to deal with. But he stopped anyway.

The gray cat had a broken leg. When the veterinary technician brought him out he was sporting a large splint. Mr. Vinsley paid the bill and left with the cat. Even though he didn't understand why, he felt a tug at his heart when he held the cat in his arms.

Three weeks into this new relationship, Mr. Vinsley's health took a serious turn for the worse and he was confined to his bed. The cat, by now named "Dancer"—because he could move so gracefully despite his heavy splint—left his side only to use his litter box and grab a generous amount of food.

The friendship grew deeper and deeper. When Mr. Vinsley was well enough, the pair would stroll around the grounds or sit in the sun. Dancer loved to sleep in Mr. Vinsley's lap as he listened to classical music or read a book.

And another thing happened. Mr. Vinsley started chatting with his neighbors about pets. They'd share stories and advice. After all these years, Mr. Vinsley was caring about other people again. Soon his neighbors became friends who would often stop by for a cup of coffee or to play cards.

As I listened to Mr. Vinsley talk about Dancer, I promised myself I'd do everything I could to fulfill his wish.

I made several trips to visit Mr. Vinsley and Dancer. We'd have tea together and talk. I loved those afternoon visits and think of them often.

After a lengthy search, I found a potential home for Dancer—a very sweet and gentle woman who had lost her husband years earlier. I thought it was a wonderful chance for Dancer to give this lonely person the same gift of love he'd given to Mr. Vinsley.

When Ruth Leeson met Mr. Vinsley and Dancer, all three of them hit it off. They spent much time together, and Mr. Vinsley took great pleasure in telling Ruth all about Dancer's likes and dislikes.

Eight months after I first met Mr. Vinsley, he was taken to the hospital. His housekeeper phoned to tell me that Mr. Vinsley wanted me to come get Dancer and take him to his new home. I canceled my appointments for the day, then called Ruth to tell her to expect Dancer.

I drove to the Vinsley residence. The housekeeper let me in and I collected Dancer's things. As if he knew what was about to happen, Dancer was waiting for me in Mr. Vinsley's room. He sat quietly on the bed.

The housekeeper walked me to my car. She touched my arm and thanked me for helping Mr. Vinsley. There were tears in her eyes. She'd worked for him for fifteen years.

Later that day I visited Mr. Vinsley in the hospital to tell him that Dancer was in his new home and that Ruth was doing everything she could to make him feel at home. He smiled. We talked a little while longer and then he drifted off to sleep. I quietly got up and stood by the bed for a few moments. "I'll keep watch over Dancer for you," I whispered, and left him to rest.

Two days later Mr. Vinsley died.

I've since visited Dancer in his new home several times, and he's very happy. He follows Ruth the same way he did Mr. Vinsley. And I've noticed that Ruth looks much more content than when I first met her. She proudly told me that Dancer sleeps on his own pillow next to her in bed.

Dancer, the once scruffy, tough, stray cat, taught Mr. Vinsley how to love again. And now, the furry gray teacher with torn ears and a purr like an old car engine is helping Ruth to learn that same lesson.

Final Thoughts

For some of us, cats are graceful creatures, loyal companions, and the most intuitive friends in our lives. Yet, for others of us, cats are frustrating mysteries, a tiger in tabby's clothing and as unbending as that big oak tree in the yard. I hope this book has helped ease some of the frustration for those cat owners who feel that every day is a battle against that four-legged ball of fluff who looks like an angel and acts like a devil. Do you ever wonder what our cats think of us? I wonder if they find us to be confusing, moody, scary, and unpredictable giants? I have a feeling that we frustrate them more than they could ever frustrate us.

In our relationship with our cats, they are the ones who do most of the compromising and adapting to our rules even when those rules don't make any sense to them. Cats give so effortlessly we sometimes take it for granted.

In the wild, a cat has a few simple requirements: water, a mate (if they're lucky), a tree or two for marking and climbing, a little soil for those "personal" functions, and a modest supply of prey to catch. Then we come along and suddenly it's *"Don't climb there... Don't scratch on that... Don't pee there... Don't chase that thing...Don't be a cat!"*

Remember, look at your world through your cat's eyes and you'll find solutions to behavior problems and ways to increase the quality of his life. Positive behavior modification wins hands down every time over discipline and punishment.

If you feel you are unable to handle a behavior problem, there is a lot of help out there for you. Consult with your vet. S/he can then refer you to a behaviorist if needed. Behaviorists are available for housecalls, phone consultations, or clinic appointments.

It's a cat's life...make it a good one!

Index

A

Abnormal behaviors, 10-11
Aggression, 7, 47-78. *See also* Furniture scratching
analyzing, 48, 75
extreme, 11
playing at, 75-77
redirected, 9, 59-68
unprovoked, 124
Amitriptyline, 56, 58
Animals, problems with other, 15-22, 53, 59-68, 95-99, 125. *See also* Aggression, redirected
Anxiety, 74, 79-80, 111-126, 140
Avoidance behaviors, 8, 88

B

Baby gate, using, 21
Behaviorists. *See* Feline behavior consultants
Behavior modification, positive, 8, 156
Behavior problems, 6. *See also* Aggression; Litter box problems; other individual problems
normal versus abnormal, 10-11
positive solutions to, 9, 76
Birdbaths, 91
Biting. *See* Aggression
Black light, using, 20, 26-28, 93
Boredom. *See* Restlessness

Boxes, uses for, 20, 22, 64
Breeds mentioned
Abyssinian, 124
Burmese, 127
Himalayan, 124, 127
Manx, 38
Siamese, 111-127
Tonkinese, 127
Bribery, 66-68

C

Cardboard scratching pads, 89, 98-99
Carpet, cats' reactions to, 37-46, 82
Carriers, 73-74, 77-78, 113
top-loading, 78
Cat owners
avoiding veterinarians, 117-119
equipment for, 10
Cats
communicating with, 8, 48, 145
euthanizing, 6
as family members, 140
geriatric, 35
getting to play, 61
hatred of change, 36
language of, 9
learning from, 145
mourning, 134-145
need for cover, 64
need for familiar territory, 52-57
normal behavior of, 10-11
not battling with, 44, 52, 56
obesity in, 34-35
observing, 24-26, 40-41, 90

predatory nature of, 29, 63, 122
requirements of, 155-156
self-confident, 63-64
separating, 59-60
thinking like, 5-6, 155-156
Cat trees, 21-22, 57-58, 76, 83, 93-94, 108, 125-126
Change
cats' hatred of, 36
emotional effects of, 14, 40
Clawing. *See* Declawing
Comfort zone, 64
Communicating with cats, 8, 48-49, 145
Companion cat, 108, 110
Compulsions, 127-133
Confidence-building. *See* Self-confidence in cats
Cravings, 127-133
Crises, emotional effects of, 14
Curtains, cats' reactions to, 123, 125

D

Declawing, 79-80, 85, 87
problems connected with, 41, 80
Defensive behavior. *See* Aggression
Diet, 34-35, 126, 131, 133
Discipline, counterproductive, 8, 13, 29, 89, 156
Diversions, 65-66, 92, 131

E

Elimination, inappropriate. *See* Litter box problems
Emotional upset, causes of, 14
Enzyme cleaners, using, 20, 46, 122
Euthanizing, 6, 48, 69, 72, 77, 130, 135

F

Family counseling, 69-78
Fascinations, 101-110
Faucets, fascination with, 101-110
Fear, 8, 29, 63, 73
Feline behavior consultants, 6, 11, 14, 30, 48, 146, 148, 156
Feline Hyperesthesia Syndrome, 124
Felix Post, 87, 90
FELV/FIV, testing for, 117
Fish tank, 108-110
Food
  home-cooked, 34-35
  marking nest areas with, 28
Frustration, 65, 155
Furniture scratching, 11, 79-99

G

Grieving, 134-145
Grooming, 76-77
Group play therapy, 68

H

Hairballs, medication for, 46
"Hello" visits to vet, 74, 78
Hitting cats, 7-8
Home-cooked food, 34-35

Hyperesthesia. *See* Feline Hyperesthesia Syndrome

I

Influencing cats, 6
Interactive toys, 9-10, 28-29, 58, 61, 64-66, 75-77, 89, 110, 122, 145

K

Kitty Kreek, 109

L

Litter box problems, handling, 10-11, 13-46
  adding a second box, 21-22, 30, 33, 63
  box rejection, 23, 30
  brand or type of litter, 41, 46
  encouraging box use, 28
  proper location for, 25-26
  providing adequate boxes, 32, 34
  scooping routine, 33-35
Love, unconditional, 145-154
Lunging behavior, 111-126
LUTD (Lower Urinary Tract Disease). *See* Urinary problems

M

Males
  spraying, 44
  urinary problems of, 14
Medical problems, 13-14. *See also* individual medical problems
Medication, 54, 56-58, 62, 67, 78, 107, 126

Milk tread, 127
Misbehavior. *See* Behavior problems
MRI on cats, 124
Multi-pet homes, 15-22, 95-99. *See also* Territory, controlling

N

Negative situations, making positive, 9, 76
Normal behavior, defining, 10-11, 90
Nose, rubbing in accidents, 7-8
Nutrition. *See* Diet

O

Obsessions, 101-110. *See also* Compulsions
Obsessive-Compulsive Disorder (OCD), 128, 132
Odors, neutralizing, 20, 28
Owners. *See* Cat owners

P

Pain, 13
Pecking order, 96-97
Pets
  mourning for another pet, 134-145
  problems with other, 15-22, 53, 59-68, 95-99
Physical punishment. *See* Punishment
Play aggression, 75-77
Play therapy, 9, 22, 28-29, 32, 34-35, 92, 144
  group, 68
  specific instructions, 65
  time and place for, 10, 64

Predatory instinct, 122
  taking advantage of,
  29, 63
Problems. *See also*
  Aggression; Litter
  box problems; other
  individual problems
  list of common, 36
Products recommended
  Felix Post, 87, 90
  Kitty Kreek, 109
  Prozac, 107, 132
Punishment, 7-8, 29,
  131, 156

Q

Questionnaire, 49-50

R

Restlessness, 93-94,
  107-110, 138

S

Scent, transferring, 98-
  99
Scratching. *See* Aggres-
  sion; Declawing;
  Furniture scratching
Scratching posts.
  See also Cat trees
  horizontal versus
  vertical, 88-90
  making, 82
  positioning, 83, 93-94,
  97-99

pre-scenting, 98-99
  selecting, 81-82
Self-confidence in cats,
  63-65
Shedding, 72, 76
Showers, fascination
  with, 103-106
Skin twitching, 116-119,
  122-124
Spitefulness, 23
Spraying
  mock, 92-93
  versus urinating, 44
Stains, removing, 20, 28
Stalking behavior, 10,
  60, 65
Strays, working with,
  42-44
Stress. *See* Anxiety
Sucking behavior, 127-
  133

T

Tail twitching, 92-94
Tension, 8. *See also*
  Aggression; Anxiety
Territory, controlling,
  52-57, 79
Toys. *See* Interactive
  toys
Trainers, consulting, 5,
  22, 141, 143
Tranquilizers. *See*
  Medications; individ-
  ual tranquilizers
Treatment plans, 7

Treats, what to feed, 66
Twisted Whiskers:
  Solving Your Cat's
  Behavior Problems, 9

U

Urinary problems, 13-
  14, 92
Urine spots, detecting,
  20, 26-28, 93

V

Vaccinations, 78, 117
Valium, 54, 56
Veterinarians, 6-7, 11,
  14, 23, 30, 48-49, 84-
  87, 92, 141, 156. *See*
  also Medication
  cats' fear of, 69-78
  "hello" visits to, 74, 78
  housecalls, requesting,
  78

W

Water, fascination with,
  101-110
Weaning, premature,
  127
Wool sucking, 127-133

BOOKS BY THE CROSSING PRESS

Bark Busters
Solving Your Dog's Behavioral Problems
By Sylvia Wilson

This step-by-step guide will help you improve your relationship with your pet. The techniques are designed to work with a dog's natural instincts, without cruelty.
$12.95 • Paper • ISBN 0-89594-881-8

The Holistic Puppy
How to Have a Happy, Healthy Dog
By Diane Stein

Diane Stein shares her experience and gives useful information about choosing a dog and bringing it home, behavior training, handling and grooming, nutrition, and solving the dog's emotional problems.
$14.95 • Paper • ISBN 0-89594-946-6

Natural Healing for Dogs and Cats
By Diane Stein

This invaluable resource tells how to use nutrition, minerals, massage, herbs, homeopathy, acupuncture, acupressure, flower essences, and psychic healing for optimal health.
$16.95 • Paper • ISBN 0-89594-614-9

The Natural Remedy Book for Dogs & Cats
By Diane Stein

"An informative guide to the use of nutrition, vitamins, massage, herbs, and homeopathy to support your pet's health and vitality. Sure to be effective in reducing veterinary costs, while enhancing your relationship with your furry loved one."—NAPRA Trade Journal
$16.95 • Paper • ISBN 0-89594-686-6

Twisted Whiskers
Solving Your Cat's Behavior Problems
By Pam Johnson

"Johnson's cat-friendly, no-nonsense techniques glow with common sense and insight...a practical guide and an inspiration."
$12.95 • Paper • ISBN 0-89594-710-2

To receive a current catalog from The Crossing Press
please call toll-free, 800-777-1048.
Visit our Web site on the Internet: www. crossingpress.com